Table of Contents

Table of Contents

Name: _____

Place Value

The place value of a digit or numeral is shown by where it is in the number. In the number 1,234, 1 has the place value of thousands, 2 is hundreds, 3 is tens and 4 is ones.

Example: 1,250,000,000

Read: One billion, two hundred fifty million

Write: 1,250,000,000

Billions			Millions			Thousands			Ones		
h	t	o	h	t	o	h	t	o	h	t	o
		1,		2	5	0,	0	0	0,	0	0	0

Directions: Read the words. Then write the numbers.

twenty million, three hundred four thousand ___20_____

five thousand, four hundred twenty-three ___5 4 2 3_____

one hundred fifty billion, eight million,
one thousand, five hundred _____

sixty billion, seven hundred million,
one hundred thousand, three hundred twelve _____

four hundred million, fifteen thousand,
seven hundred one _____

six hundred ninety-nine million, four thousand,
nine hundred forty-two _____

Here's a game to play with a partner.

Write a ten-digit number using each digit, 0 to 9, only once. Do not show the number to your partner. Give clues like: "There is a five in the hundreds place." The clues can be given in any order. See if your partner can write the same number you have written.

Place Value

Directions: Draw a line to connect each number to its correct written form.

1. 791,000   Three hundred fifty thousand

2. 350,000   Seventeen million, five hundred thousand

3. 17,500,000   Seven hundred ninety-one thousand

4. 3,500,000   Seventy thousand, nine hundred ten

5. 70,910   Three million, five hundred thousand

6. 35,500,000   Seventeen billion, five hundred thousand

7. 17,000,500,000   Thirty-five million, five hundred thousand

Directions: Look carefully at this number: 2,071,463,548. Write the numeral for each of the following places.

8. _____ ten thousands

9. _____ millions

10. _____ hundreds

11. _____ billions

12. _____ hundred thousands

13. _____ ten millions

14. _____ one thousands

15. _____ hundred millions

Name: _____

Addition

Addition is "putting together" two or more numbers to find the sum.

Directions: Add. Fill the backpacks with the right answers.

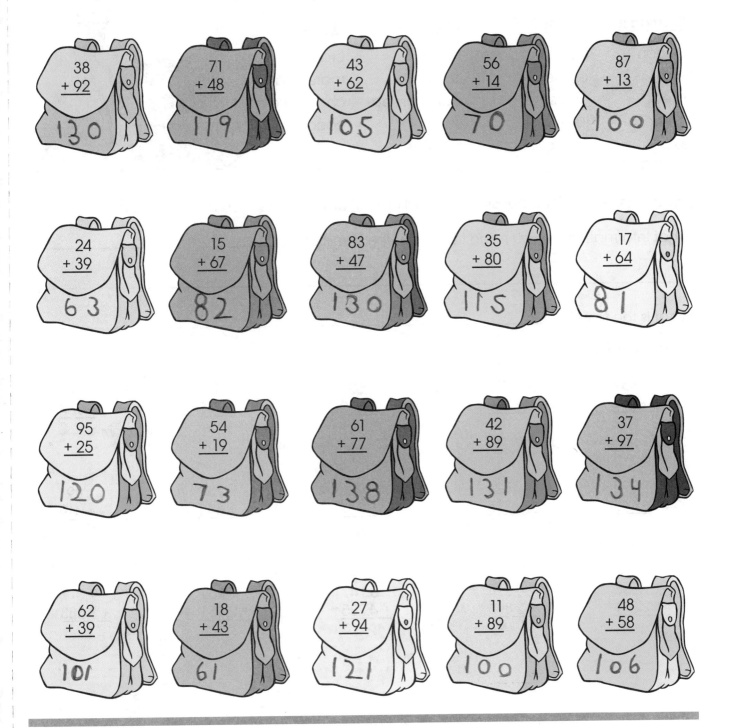

38
+ 92
130

71
+ 48
119

43
+ 62
105

56
+ 14
70

87
+ 13
100

24
+ 39
63

15
+ 67
82

83
+ 47
130

35
+ 80
115

17
+ 64
81

95
+ 25
120

54
+ 19
73

61
+ 77
138

42
+ 89
131

37
+ 97
134

62
+ 39
101

18
+ 43
61

27
+ 94
121

11
+ 89
100

48
+ 58
106

Name: _____

Addition

Teachers of an Earth Science class planned to take 50 students on an overnight hiking and camping experience. After planning the menu, they went to the grocery store for supplies.

Breakfast	Lunch	Dinner	Snacks
bacon	hot dogs/buns	pasta	crackers
eggs	apples	sauce	marshmallows
bread	chips	garlic bread	chocolate bars
cereal	juice	salad	cocoa mix
juice	granola bars	cookies	
$34.50	$ 52.15	$ 47.25	$ 23.40

Directions: Answer the questions. Write the total amount spent on food for the trip.

What information do you need to answer the question? _____

_____

What is the total? _____

Directions: Add.

$$\begin{array}{r} 462 \\ + 574 \\ \hline 1036 \end{array} \qquad \begin{array}{r} 918 \\ + 359 \\ \hline 1277 \end{array} \qquad \begin{array}{r} 527 \\ + 582 \\ \hline 1109 \end{array} \qquad \begin{array}{r} 386 \\ + 745 \\ \hline 1131 \end{array} \qquad \begin{array}{r} 295 \\ + 764 \\ \hline 1059 \end{array}$$

$$\begin{array}{r} 397 \\ + 448 \\ \hline 845 \end{array} \qquad \begin{array}{r} 524 \\ + 725 \\ \hline 1249 \end{array} \qquad \begin{array}{r} 906 \\ + 337 \\ \hline 1243 \end{array} \qquad \begin{array}{r} 750 \\ + 643 \\ \hline 1393 \end{array} \qquad \begin{array}{r} 891 \\ + 419 \\ \hline 1310 \end{array}$$

$$\begin{array}{r} 1{,}568 \\ + 2{,}341 \\ \hline 3909 \end{array} \qquad \begin{array}{r} 3{,}214 \\ + 2{,}896 \\ \hline 6110 \end{array} \qquad \begin{array}{r} 5{,}147 \\ + 4{,}285 \\ \hline 9432 \end{array} \qquad \begin{array}{r} 7{,}259 \\ + 2{,}451 \\ \hline 9710 \end{array} \qquad \begin{array}{r} 9{,}317 \\ + 3{,}583 \\ \hline 12900 \end{array}$$

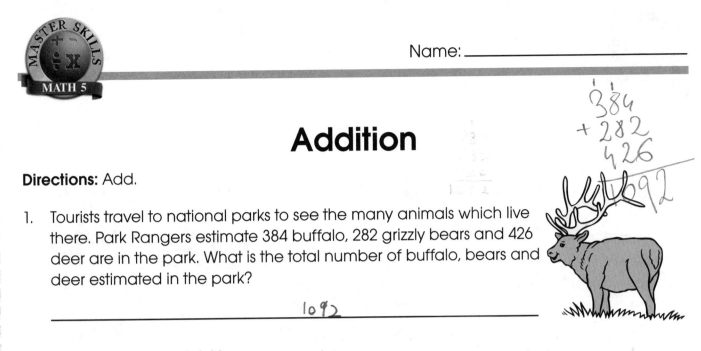

$$\begin{array}{r} \overset{1}{3}\overset{1}{8}4 \\ + 282 \\ \hline 426 \\ \end{array}$$

1092

Addition

Directions: Add.

1. Tourists travel to national parks to see the many animals which live there. Park Rangers estimate 384 buffalo, 282 grizzly bears and 426 deer are in the park. What is the total number of buffalo, bears and deer estimated in the park?

   _____ 1092 _____

2. Last August, 2,248 visitors drove motor homes into the campgrounds for overnight camping. 647 set up campsites with tents. How many campsites were there altogether in August?

   _____

3. During a 3-week camping trip, Tom and his family hiked 42 miles, took a 126 mile long canoeing trip and drove their car 853 miles. How many miles did they travel in all?

   _____

4. Old Faithful is a geyser which spouts water high into the air. 10,000 gallons of water burst into the air regularly. Two other geysers spout 2,400 gallons of water during each eruption. What is the amount of water thrust into the air during one cycle?

   _____

5. Yellowstone National Park covers approximately 2,221,772 acres of land. Close by, the Grand Tetons cover approximately 310,350 acres. How many acres of land are there in these two parks?

   _____

6. Hiking trails cover 486 miles, motor routes around the north rim total 376 miles, and another 322 miles of road allow visitors to follow a loop around the southern part of the park. How many miles of trails and roadways are there?

   _____

Addition

Directions: Circle the lilypads with the correct answers to show the frogs the correct path to follow to join their mother on the other side of the pond.

52,913
+ 21,727
73,630

327
+ 418
735

14,525
+ 11,607
25,122

486
+ 583
964

74
+ 37
111

1,197
+ 423
1,520

375
+ 425
800

83,159
+ 12,432
95,581

73,482
+ 23,435
96,817

65,219
+ 25,098
90,317

870
+ 230
1,100

754
+ 347
1,091

26,492
+ 35,218
51,600

765
+ 245
1,010

49,639
+ 7,421
57,060

4,217
+ 12,982
17,199

8,951
+ 1,649
10,500

Name: _____

Addition

Bob the butcher is popular with the dogs in town. He was making a delivery this morning when he noticed he was being followed by two dogs. Bob tried to climb a ladder to escape from the dogs. Solve the following addition problems and shade in the answers on the ladder. If all the numbers are shaded when the problems have been solved, Bob made it up the ladder. Some answers may not be on the ladder.

1.
```
    986,145
    621,332
 +  200,008
  ─────────
  1807485
```

2.
```
  1,873,402
    925,666
 +    4,689
  ─────────
  2803757
```

3.
```
    506,328
    886,510
 +  342,225
  ─────────
  1735063
```

4.
```
     43,015
  2,811,604
 +  987,053
  ─────────
  3841672
```

5.
```
     18,443
    300,604
 +  999,999
  ─────────
  1319046
```

6.
```
      8,075
     14,608
 +   33,914
  ─────────
     56597
```

7.
```
      9,162
      7,804
 +  755,122
  ─────────
    772088
```

8.
```
     88,714
    213,653
 + 5,441,298
  ─────────
   5643665
```

9.
```
  3,244,662
  1,986,114
 +  521,387
  ─────────
  5752163
```

10.
```
      4,581
     22,983
 + 5,618,775
  ─────────
  5646339
```

11.
```
    818,623
        926
 + 3,260,004
  ─────────
   4078553
```

12.
```
     80,436
      9,159
 + 3,028,761
  ─────────
  3118356
```

Ladder:
- 1,319,046
- 2,803,757
- 5,743,665
- 3,118,356
- 56,597
- 4,079,553
- 1,807,485
- 2,943,230
- 18,344,666
- 1,735,063
- 5,752,163
- 896,316
- 3,841,672
- 5,646,339

Does Bob make it? __yes__

Name: _____

Subtraction

Subtraction is "taking away" one number from another to find the difference between the two numbers.

Directions: Subtract.

```
   76          93          68          49          88          54
 - 23        - 14        - 25        - 17        - 39        - 25
   53          79          43          32          59          29
```

Brent saved $75.00 of the money he earned delivering the local newspaper in his neighborhood. He wanted to buy a new bicycle that cost $139.00. How much more would he need to save in order to buy the bike?

$64

```
   38          74          67          92          43          85
 - 29        - 25        - 49        - 35        - 26        - 37
    9          49          18          57          17          458
```

When Brent finally went to buy the bicycle, he saw a light and basket for the bike. He decided to buy them both. The light was $5.95 and the basket was $10.50. He gave the clerk a twenty dollar bill his grandmother had given him for his birthday. How much change did he get back?

$3.95

Subtraction

When working with larger numbers, it is important to keep the numbers lined up according to place value.

Subtract.

$$
\begin{array}{r} \overset{8,}{3\overset{9}{\cancel{9}}8} \\ -\ 149 \\ \hline 249 \end{array}
\qquad
\begin{array}{r} \overset{4\ \ 3.}{5\cancel{4}3} \\ -\ 287 \\ \hline 256 \end{array}
\qquad
\begin{array}{r} 491 \\ -\ 311 \\ \hline 180 \end{array}
$$

$$
\begin{array}{r} \overset{18}{6}\ \overset{}{786}\,16 \\ -\ 597 \\ \hline 199 \end{array}
\qquad
\begin{array}{r} 1,825 \\ -\ 495 \\ \hline \end{array}
\qquad
\begin{array}{r} 4,172 \\ -\ 2,785 \\ \hline \end{array}
$$

$$
\begin{array}{r} 8,391 \\ -\ 5,492 \\ \hline \end{array}
\qquad
\begin{array}{r} 63,852 \\ -\ 34,765 \\ \hline \end{array}
\qquad
\begin{array}{r} 24,107 \\ -19,350 \\ \hline \end{array}
\qquad
\begin{array}{r} 52,900 \\ -\ 43,081 \\ \hline \end{array}
$$

1110

Eagle Peak is the highest mountain peak at Yellowstone National Park. It is 11,353 feet high. The next highest point at the park is Mount Washburn. It is 10,243 feet tall. How much higher is Eagle Peak?

It is 1110 higer

The highest mountain peak in North America is Mount McKinley, which stretches 20,320 feet toward the sky. Two other mountain ranges in North America have peaks at 10,302 feet and 8,194 feet. What is the greatest difference between the peaks?

Checking Subtraction

You can check your subtraction by using addition.

Example: 34,436   Check: → 22,172
             – 12,264   ⤫   → + 12,264
              22,172   →   34,436

Directions: Subtract. Then check your answers by adding.

15,326 – 11,532	Check:	28,615 – 25,329	Check:
96,521 – 47,378	Check:	46,496 – 35,877	Check:
77,911 – 63,783	Check:	156,901 –112,732	Check:
395,638 –187,569	Check:	67,002 – 53,195	Check:
16,075 –15,896	Check:	39,678 –19,769	Check:
84,654 – 49,997	Check:	12,335 –10,697	Check:

During the summer, 158,941 people visited Yellowstone National Park. During the fall, there were 52,397 visitors. How many more visitors went to the park during the summer than the fall?

_____

Name: _____

Addition and Subtraction

Directions: Check the answers. Write **T** if the answer is true and **F** if it is false. The first one has been done for you.

Example:
```
  48,973     Check:      35,856
– 35,856       F        +13,118
  13,118      ‾‾‾‾        48,974
```

```
  18,264     Check:                  458,342    Check:
+ 17,893        F                   – 297,652
  36,157      ‾‾‾‾                    160,680     ‾‾‾‾

                x
```

```
  39,854     Check:                  631,928    Check:
+ 52,713                            – 457,615
  92,577      ‾‾‾‾                    174,313     ‾‾‾‾
```

```
  14,389     Check:                  554,974    Check:
+ 93,587                            – 376,585
 107,976      ‾‾‾‾                    178,389     ‾‾‾‾
```

```
  87,321     Check:                  109,568    Check:
– 62,348                            + 97,373
  24,973      ‾‾‾‾                    206,941     ‾‾‾‾
```

Directions: Read the story problem. Write the equation and check the answer.

A camper hikes 53,741 feet out into the wilderness. On his return trip he takes a shortcut, walking 36,752 feet back to his cabin. The shortcut saves him 16,998 feet of hiking. True or False?

Name: _____

Addition and Subtraction

Directions: Add or subtract to find the answers.

Eastland School hosted a field day. Students could sign up for a variety of events. 175 students signed up for individual races. Twenty two-person teams competed in the mile relay and 36 kids took part in the high jump. How many students participated in the activities?

_____

Westmore School brought 42 students and 7 adults to the field day event. Northern School brought 84 students and 15 adults. There was a total of 300 students and 45 adults at the event. How many were from other schools?

_____

The Booster Club sponsored a concession stand during the day. Last year, they made $1,000 at the same event. This year they hoped to earn at least $1,250. They actually raised $1,842. How much more did they make than they had anticipated?

_____

Each school was awarded a trophy for participating in the field day's activities. The Booster Club planned to purchase three plaques as awards, but they only wanted to spend $150. The first place trophy they selected was $68. The second place award was $59. How much would they be able to spend on the third place award if they stay within their budgeted amount?

_____

The Booster Club decided to spend $1,000 to purchase several items for the school with the money they had earned. Study the list of items suggested and decide which combination of items they could purchase.

A. Swing set $425 _____

B. Sliding board $263 _____

C. Scoreboard $515 _____

D. Team uniforms $180 _____

14

Name: _____

Addition

When adding many numbers together, be sure to keep them lined up according to their place value.

Directions: Add. Use a calculator to check your answers.

408,107	75,310	708,302	6,700,241
31,641	89,632	40,927	9,334,300
9,111	1,542	20,085	3,017
400	736	343	4,322,119
+ 295	+ 922	+ 589	+ 7,384

215,106	3,892,442	5,312,612	8,700,370
69,015	318,712	680,325	804,304
5,446	76,698	46,659	17,009
621	7,361	7,360	7,919
+ 306	+ 567	+ 812	+ 250

954,432	6,935	12,897
126,243	12,897	64,382
27,591	69,473	29,318
8,920	43,190	13,269
+ 27	+ 48,579	+ 4,769

64,513
1,943
43,009
36,820
+ 32,692

Name: _____

Rounding

Rounding a number means to express it to the nearest ten, hundred, thousand and so on. When rounding a number to the nearest ten, if the number has five or more ones, round up. Round down if the number has four or fewer ones.

Examples:

Round to the nearest ten:	84 $\longrightarrow$	80	86 $\longrightarrow$	90
Round to the nearest hundred:	187 $\longrightarrow$	200	120 $\longrightarrow$	100
Round to the nearest thousand:	981 $\longrightarrow$	1,000	5,480 $\longrightarrow$	5,000

Directions: Round these numbers to the nearest ten.

87 → _____   53 → _____   48 → _____   32 → _____   76 → _____

Directions: Round these numbers to the nearest hundred.

168 → _____   243 → _____   591 → _____   743 → _____   493 → _____

Directions: Round these numbers to the nearest thousand.

895 → _____   3,492 → _____   7,521 → _____   14,904 → _____   62,387 → _____

City Populations	
City	Population
Cleveland	492,801
Seattle	520,947
Omaha	345,033
Kansas City	443,878
Atlanta	396,052
Austin	514,013

Directions: Use the city population chart to answer the questions.

Which cities have a population of about 500,000?

_____

Which city has a population of about 350,000?

_____

How many cities have a population of about 400,000? _____

Which ones? _____

_____

Name: _____

Estimating

To **estimate** means to give an approximate rather than an exact answer. Rounding each number first makes it easy to estimate an answer.

Example:

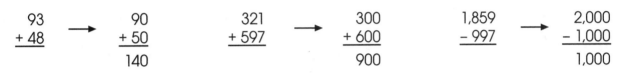

$$\begin{array}{r} 93 \\ + 48 \end{array} \rightarrow \begin{array}{r} 90 \\ + 50 \\ \hline 140 \end{array} \qquad \begin{array}{r} 321 \\ + 597 \end{array} \rightarrow \begin{array}{r} 300 \\ + 600 \\ \hline 900 \end{array} \qquad \begin{array}{r} 1,859 \\ - 997 \end{array} \rightarrow \begin{array}{r} 2,000 \\ - 1,000 \\ \hline 1,000 \end{array}$$

Directions: Estimate the sums and differences by rounding the numbers first.

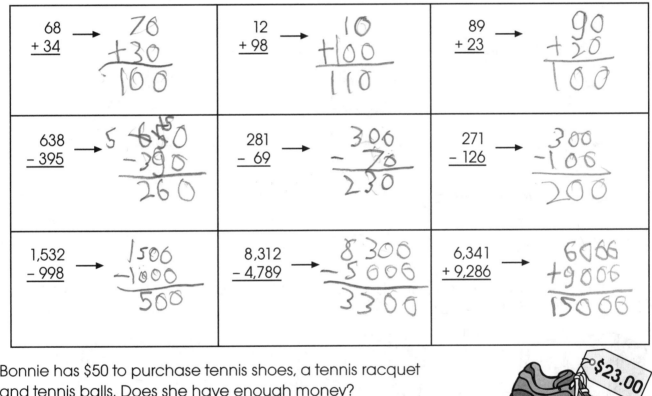

$\begin{array}{r} 68 \\ + 34 \end{array} \rightarrow$	$\begin{array}{r} 70 \\ +30 \\ \hline 100 \end{array}$	
$\begin{array}{r} 12 \\ + 98 \end{array} \rightarrow \begin{array}{r} 10 \\ +100 \\ \hline 110 \end{array}$		
$\begin{array}{r} 89 \\ + 23 \end{array} \rightarrow \begin{array}{r} 90 \\ +20 \\ \hline 100 \end{array}$		

(grid of problems:)

$\begin{array}{r} 68 \\ + 34 \end{array} \rightarrow \begin{array}{r} 70 \\ +30 \\ \hline 100 \end{array}$ $\quad$ $\begin{array}{r} 12 \\ + 98 \end{array} \rightarrow \begin{array}{r} 10 \\ +100 \\ \hline 110 \end{array}$ $\quad$ $\begin{array}{r} 89 \\ + 23 \end{array} \rightarrow \begin{array}{r} 90 \\ +20 \\ \hline 100 \end{array}$

$\begin{array}{r} 638 \\ - 395 \end{array} \rightarrow \begin{array}{r} 650 \\ -390 \\ \hline 260 \end{array}$ $\quad$ $\begin{array}{r} 281 \\ - 69 \end{array} \rightarrow \begin{array}{r} 300 \\ -70 \\ \hline 230 \end{array}$ $\quad$ $\begin{array}{r} 271 \\ - 126 \end{array} \rightarrow \begin{array}{r} 300 \\ -100 \\ \hline 200 \end{array}$

$\begin{array}{r} 1,532 \\ - 998 \end{array} \rightarrow \begin{array}{r} 1500 \\ -1000 \\ \hline 500 \end{array}$ $\quad$ $\begin{array}{r} 8,312 \\ - 4,789 \end{array} \rightarrow \begin{array}{r} 8300 \\ -5000 \\ \hline 3300 \end{array}$ $\quad$ $\begin{array}{r} 6,341 \\ + 9,286 \end{array} \rightarrow \begin{array}{r} 6000 \\ +9000 \\ \hline 15000 \end{array}$

Bonnie has $50 to purchase tennis shoes, a tennis racquet and tennis balls. Does she have enough money?

Yes   She does

$23.00

$16.00

$3.00

Name: _____

Rounding and Estimating

Rounding numbers and estimating answers is an easy way of finding the approximate answer without writing out the problem or using a calculator.

Directions: Circle the correct answer.

Round to the nearest **ten**:

73 → (70) / 80

48 → 40 / (50)

65 → 60 / (70)

85 → 80 / (90)

92 → (90) / 100

37 → 30 / (40)

Round to the nearest **hundred**:

139 → (100) / 200

782 → 700 / (800)

390 → 300 / (400)

640 → (600) / 700

525 → (500) / 600

457 → 400 / (500)

Round to the nearest **thousand**:

1,375 → (1,000) / 2,000

21,800 → 21,000 / (22,000)

36,240 → (36,000) / 37,000

Sam wanted to buy a new computer. He knew he only had about $1,200 to spend. Which of the following ones could he afford to buy?

$1,165 $1,279 $1,249

If Sam spent $39 on software for his new computer, $265 for a printer and $38 for a cordless mouse, about how much money did he need?

342   dollers

265
+ 39
3 04

Name: _____

Review

Directions: Add.

1. 45 + 50 = __95__

5. 72 + 28 = __100__

9. 92 + 18 = __110__

2. 63 + 37 = __100__

6. 56 + 16 = __62__

10. 34 + 70 = __103__

3. 25 + 60 = __85__

7. 90 + 43 = __133__

11. 75 + 75 = __150__

4. 55 + __55__ = 110

8. 63 + __63__ = 136

12. 90 + __169__ = 159

$$\begin{array}{r} 63 \\ +63 \end{array}$$

Anne ordered these items for breakfast at her favorite restaurant:

scrambled eggs

toast

orange juice

bacon strips

How much did she spend? _____

Anne paid for her breakfast with a ten-dollar bill.
How much change should she get back? _____

Specials

Eggs	$2.50
Bacon	$2.15
Toast	$1.20
Juice	$1.25

Directions: Subtract.

13. 95 – 30 = _____

17. 49 – 10 = _____

21. 88 – 20 = _____

14. 125 – 50 = _____

18. 78 – 30 = _____

22. 92 – 16 = _____

15. 67 – 20 = _____

19. 150 – 65 = _____

23. 180 – 90 = _____

16. 140 – _____ = 60

20. 185 – _____ = 95

24. 250 – _____ = 175

Name: _____

Review

Directions: Add.

256	8,968	28,493	168,573
+ 538	+ 3,481	+ 38,975	+ 257,899

Directions: Subtract.

189,453	1,350,681	856,721	29,051
- 98,794	- 467,792	- 650,853	- 15,160

Directions: Draw a line to the number that has:

five ten millions   1,950,783

six hundreds   45,640

nine hundred thousands   17,001

zero tens   1,453,682,073

Directions: Round to the nearest

ten	83 → 80	48 → 50	77 → 80
hundred	4,848 → 4800	5,443 → 5400	8,501 → 8500
thousand	2,920 → 3000	18,458 → 18000	179,642 → 180000
million	1,891,403 → _____	3,499,999 → _____	

Directions: Estimate the sums and differences by rounding.

582 →	7,951 →	6,891 →	17,988 →
+ 175	- 1,241	+ 578	- 5,749

Name: _____

Prime Numbers

Example: 3 is a prime number $3 \div 1 = 3$ and $3 \div 3 = 1$
Any other divisor will result in a mixed number
or fraction.

An easy way to test a number to see if it is prime is to divide
by 2 and 3. If the number can be divided by 2 or 3 without
a remainder, it is not a prime number. (Exceptions, 2
and 3.)

> A prime number
> is a positive whole number
> which can be divided evenly
> only by itself or one.

Example:

11 cannot be divided evenly by 2 or 3. It can only be divided by 1
and 11. It is a prime number.

Directions: Write the first 15 prime numbers. Test by dividing by 2
and by 3.

Prime Numbers:

_____   _____   _____   _____   _____

_____   _____   _____   _____   _____

_____   _____   _____   _____   _____

How many prime numbers are there between 0 and 100? _____

Name: _____

Prime Numbers

Directions: Circle the prime numbers.

71	3	82	20	43	69
128	97	23	111	75	51
13	44	137	68	171	83
61	21	77	101	34	16
2	39	92	17	52	29
19	156	63	99	27	147
121	25	88	12	87	55
57	7	139	91	9	37
67	183	5	59	11	95

Multiples

A **multiple** is the product of a specific number and any other number. When you multiply two numbers, the answer is called the **product**.

Example:

The multiples of 2 are 2 (2 x 1), 4 (2 x 2), 6, 8, 10, 12, and so on.

The **least common multiple** (LCM) of two or more numbers is the smallest number other than 0 that is a multiple of each number.

Example:

Multiples of 3 are 3, 6, 9, 12, 15, 18, 21, 24, etc.
Multiples of 6 are 6, 12, 18, 24, 30, 36, 42, etc.
The multiples that 3 and 6 have in common are 6, 12, 18, 24.
The LCM of 3 and 6 is 6.

Directions: Write the first nine multiples of 3, 4, and 6. Write the LCM.

3: _____ , _____ , _____ , _____ , _____ , _____ , _____ , _____ , _____

4: _____ , _____ , _____ , _____ , _____ , _____ , _____ , _____ , _____

6: _____ , _____ , _____ , _____ , _____ , _____ , _____ , _____ , _____

LCM = _____

Directions: Write the first nine multiples of 2 and 5. Write the LCM.

2: _____ , _____ , _____ , _____ , _____ , _____ , _____ , _____ , _____

5: _____ , _____ , _____ , _____ , _____ , _____ , _____ , _____ , _____

LCM = _____

Directions: Find the LCM for each pair of numbers.

7 and 3 _____   4 and 6 _____   6 and 9 _____

5 and 15 _____   5 and 4 _____   3 and 18 _____

Directions: Fill in the missing numbers.

30 has multiples of 5 and _____ , of 2 and _____ , of 3 and _____ .

Name: _____

Factors

Factors are the numbers multiplied together to give a product. The **greatest common factor** (GCF) is the largest number for a set of numbers that divides evenly into each number in the set.

Example:

The factors of 12 are 3 x 4, 2 x 6 and 1 x 12.

We can write the factors like this: 3, 4, 2, 6, 12, 1.

The factors of 8 are 2, 4, 8, 1.

The common factors of 12 and 8 are 2 and 4 and 1.

The GCF of 12 and 8 is 4.

Directions: Write the factors of each pair of numbers. Then write the common factors and the GCF.

12: _____ , _____ , _____ , _____ , _____ , _____

15: _____ , _____ , _____ , _____

The common factors of 12 and 15 are _____ , _____ .

The GCF is _____ .

20: _____ , _____ , _____ , _____ , _____ , _____

10: _____ , _____ , _____ , _____

The common factors of 10 and 20 are _____ , _____ , _____ , _____ .

The GCF is _____ .

32: _____ , _____ , _____ , _____ , _____ , _____

24: _____ , _____ , _____ , _____ , _____ , _____ , _____

The common factors of 24 and 32 are _____ , _____ , _____ , _____ .

The GCF is _____ .

Directions: Write the GCF for the following pairs of numbers.

28 and 20 _____   42 and 12 _____

36 and 12 _____   20 and 5 _____

Factor Trees

A **factor tree** shows the prime factors of a number. A prime number, such as 7, has for its factors only itself and 1.

Example:

```
       30
      6 x 5     30 = 3 x 2 x 5.

     3   2   5    3, 2, and 5 are prime numbers.
```

Directions: Fill in the numbers in the factor trees.

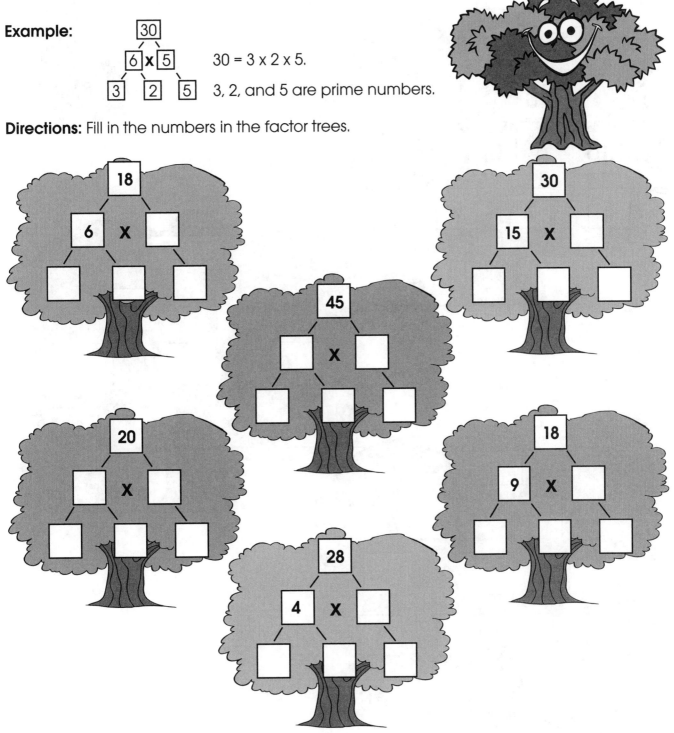

Name: _____

Factor Trees

Directions: Fill in the numbers in the factor trees. The first one has been done for you.

Name: _____

Greatest Common Factor

Directions: Write the greatest common factor for each set of numbers.

10 and 35 _____

2 and 10 _____

42 and 63 _____

16 and 40 _____

25 and 55 _____

12 and 20 _____

14 and 28 _____

8 and 20 _____

6 and 27 _____

15 and 35 _____

18 and 48 _____

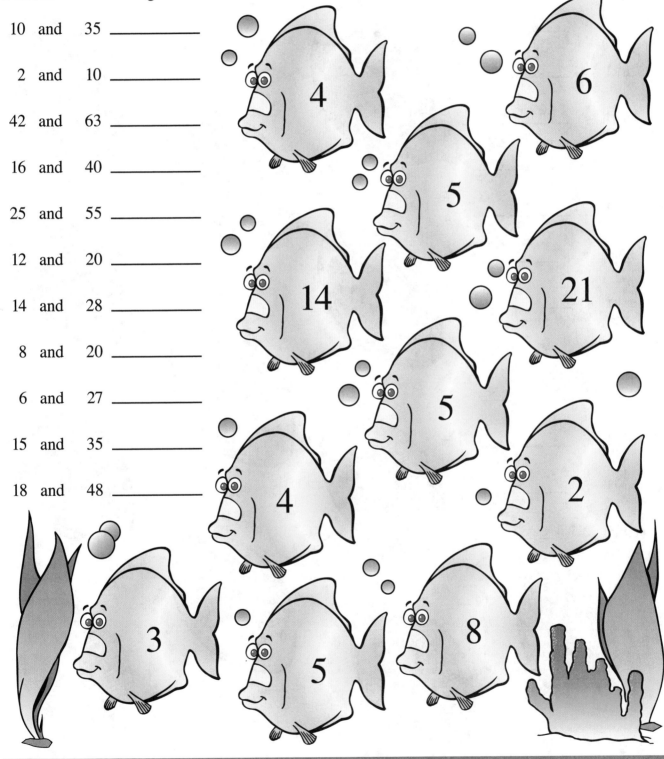

Name: _____

Least Common Multiple

Directions: Write the least common multiple for each pair of numbers.

12 and 7 _____

2 and 4 _____

22 and 4 _____

6 and 10 _____

3 and 7 _____

6 and 8 _____

5 and 10 _____

8 and 12 _____

9 and 15 _____

7 and 5 _____

3 and 8 _____

9 and 4 _____

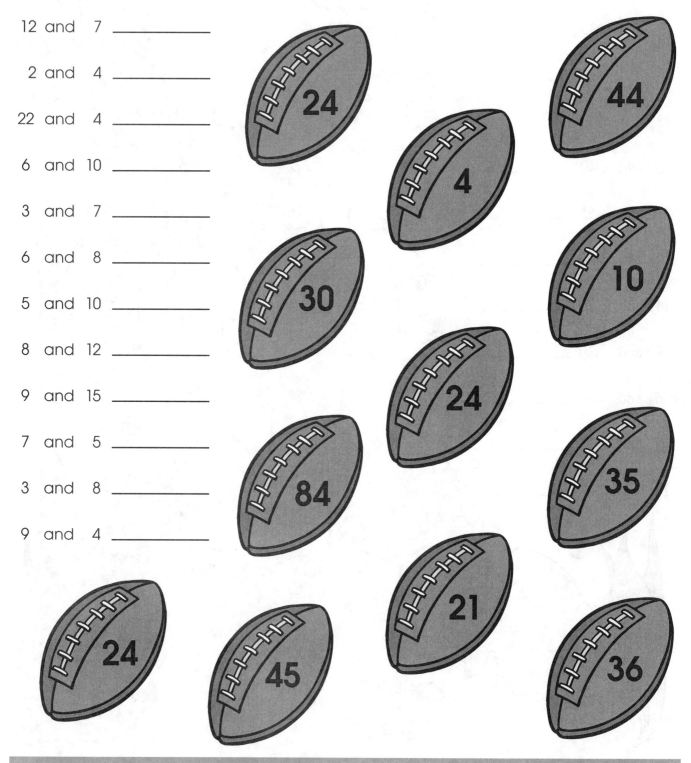

Name: _KAROL_

Multiplication

Multiplication is a process of quick addition of a number a certain number of times.

Example: 3 x 15 = 45   is the same as adding   15 + 15 + 15 = 45
15 three times.

Directions: Multiply.

```
    32          ⁵48          ⁷26         ⁵19          63
  x  3         x  7        x   5        x  6        x  2
    96          337         130          116         126
```

```
  ²251         523         ¹915        ²431         ²¹275
  x  4        x  8        x   3        x  7         x  3
   1004                    2745         3017          825
```

```
   412         643         526         ²¹742
  x  21       x  17       x  22       x  35
                                       3710
                                     + 2226
                                      25970
```

```
   256         874         ³372         ²951
  x  74       x  15       x  45        x  34
                          1860          3464
                        + 1488        +2753
                         16740         30934
```

Cathy is on the cross country team. She runs 3 miles every day except
on her birthday. How many miles does she run each year?

_____

Name: _____

Multiplication

Directions: Multiply.

Josh decided to join a book club. He received a new book every 2 weeks. He read 40 pages every night during the first 2 weeks in order to finish one book. How many pages did he read?

_____

During the summer, he received 10 books in all. He read a total of 2,600 pages that summer. He read 65 pages each day that he read. How many days did it take him to read all 10 books?

_____

The book company offered him a special deal. He could purchase five books for $49.00. He decided to buy 25 books at this special price. How much money did he need to send with his order?

_____

At the end of the year, Josh decided to share his books with a friend. His friend offered to pay him $3.00 for each book, but he only had $85.00 to spend. How many books could he buy?

_____

Josh decided to join the book club for a second year. He challenged himself to read twice as many pages during the second summer. How many pages would he need to read?

_____

247	483	826	359	735
x 15	x 72	x 43	x 58	x 21

Name: KAROL

Multiplication

Be certain to keep the proper place value when multiplying by tens and hundreds.

Examples:

```
      143
    x 262
      286
      858
      286
   37,466
```

```
      250
    x 150
      000
     1250
      250
   37,500
```

Directions: Multiply.

```
      701
    x 308
     5508
   +2103
   26538
```

```
      621
    x 538
     2568
      63
```

```
      348
    x 200
```

```
      597
    x 424
```

```
      537
    x 189
```

```
      416
    x 727
```

```
      682
    x 472
```

```
      180
    x 340
```

```
      878
    x 638
```

```
      267
    x 196
```

```
      893
    x 214
```

```
      907
    x 428
```

An airplane flies 720 trips a year between the cities of Chicago and Columbus. Each trip is 375 miles. How many miles does the airplane fly each year?

Division

Division is the reverse of multiplication. It is the process of dividing a number into equal groups of smaller numbers.

Directions: Divide.

Greg had 936 marbles to share with his two brothers. If the boys divided them evenly, how many will each one get? _____

The marbles Greg kept were four different colors: blue, green, red and orange. He had the same number of each color. He divided them into two groups. One group had only orange marbles. The rest of the marbles were in the other group. How many marbles did he have in each group? orange _____ others _____

The **dividend** is the number to be divided by another number. In the problem 28 ÷ 7 = 4, 28 is the dividend.

The **divisor** is the number by which another number is divided. In the problem 28 ÷ 7 = 4, 7 is the divisor.

The **quotient** is the answer in a division problem. In the problem 28 ÷ 7 = 4, 4 is the quotient.

The **remainder** is the number left over in the quotient of a division problem. In the problem 29 ÷ 7 = 4 r1, 1 is the remainder.

Directions: Write the answers.

In the problem 25 ÷ 8 = 3 r1 . . .

What is the divisor? _____ What is the remainder? _____

What is the quotient? _____ What is the dividend? _____

Directions: Divide.

$$9\overline{)2{,}025} \qquad 6\overline{)2{,}508} \qquad 3\overline{)225} \qquad 5\overline{)400} \qquad 2\overline{)1{,}156}$$

Name: _____

Division

When dividing with remainders, the remainder must always be less than the divisor.

Example:

```
        244 r 23
   26 )6,367
        5 2
        116
        104
        127
        104
         23
```

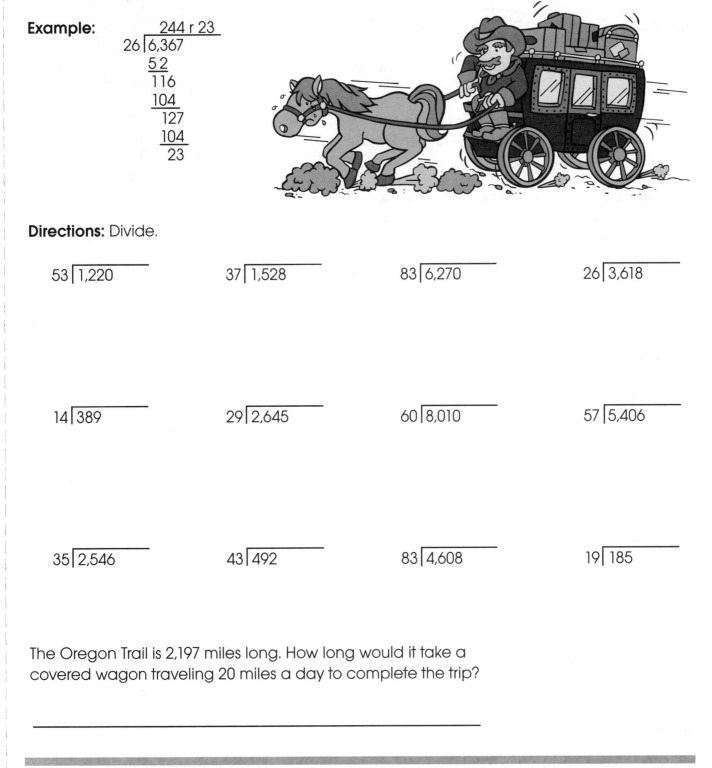

Directions: Divide.

53)1,220   37)1,528   83)6,270   26)3,618

14)389   29)2,645   60)8,010   57)5,406

35)2,546   43)492   83)4,608   19)185

The Oregon Trail is 2,197 miles long. How long would it take a
covered wagon traveling 20 miles a day to complete the trip?

_____

Name: _____

Checking Division

Answers in division problems can be checked by multiplying.

Example:

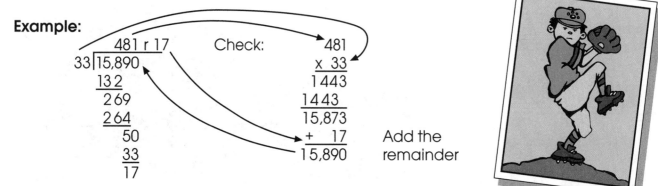

```
        481 r 17      Check:        481
  33 ) 15,890                      x  33
       13 2                         1443
        2 69                       14 43
        2 64                       15,873
           50                     +    17      Add the
           33                       15,890     remainder
           17
```

Directions: Divide and check your answers.

61) 2,736 Check:	73) 86,143 Check:
59) 9,390 Check:	43) 77,141 Check:
33) 82,050 Check:	93) 84,039 Check:

Denny has a baseball card collection. He has 13,789 cards. He wants to put the cards in a scrapbook that holds 15 cards on a page. How many pages does Denny need in his scrapbook? _____

Name: _____

Equations

An **equation** is a number sentence. To solve an equation, always work from left to right unless numbers are in parentheses.

Directions: Write the answers to these equations. The first one has been done for you.

3 **X** 2 **+** 4 **+** 9 = <u> 19 </u>

4 **X** 2 **X** 8 ÷ 4 **X** 2 = _____

9 ÷ 3 **X** 5 **X** 5 **X** 2 = _____

7 **X** 4 **X** 3 ÷ 12 **X** 8 = _____

20 **X** 3 ÷ 6 **X** 4 ÷ 5 = _____

32 ÷ 8 **X** 4 **X** 4 ÷ 2 = _____

14 ÷ 7 **X** 21 **X** 3 ÷ 3 = _____

52 **X** 5 **X** 2 ÷ 5 **X** 7 = _____

Name: _____

Multiplication and Division

Directions: Multiply or divide to find the answers.

Brianne's summer job is mowing lawns for three of her neighbors. Each lawn takes about 1 hour to mow and needs to be done once every week. At the end of the summer, she will have earned a total of $630. She collected the same amount of money from each job. How much did each neighbor pay for her summer lawn service?

_____

If the mowing season lasts for 14 weeks, how much will Brianne earn for each job each week? _____

If she had worked for two more weeks, how much would she have earned? _____

Brianne agreed to shovel snow from the driveways and sidewalks for the same three neighbors. They agreed to pay her the same rate. However, it only snowed seven times that winter. How much did she earn shoveling snow? _____

What was her total income for both jobs? _____

Directions: Multiply or divide.

$$12 \overline{)\,7{,}476}$$ $$23 \overline{)\,21{,}620}$$ $$40 \overline{)\,32{,}600}$$

32 x 45 = _____   28 x 15 = _____   73 x 14 = _____   92 x 30 = _____

Review

Directions: Write the **LCM** of each pair of numbers.

5 and 6 _____   2 and 6 _____

7 and 4 _____   4 and 8 _____

8 and 3 _____   9 and 3 _____

Directions: Write the **GCF** of each pair of numbers.

12 and 9 _____   18 and 9 _____

2 and 10 _____   27 and 3 _____

5 and 15 _____   32 and 8 _____

Directions: Multiply.

$$\begin{array}{r} 836 \\ \times\,329 \\ \hline \end{array} \qquad \begin{array}{r} 537 \\ \times\,248 \\ \hline \end{array} \qquad \begin{array}{r} 916 \\ \times\,35 \\ \hline \end{array} \qquad \begin{array}{r} 7{,}328 \\ \times\,468 \\ \hline \end{array}$$

Directions: Divide and check your answers.

$27\,\overline{)\,8{,}236}$ Check:	$93\,\overline{)\,27{,}945}$ Check:

Name: _____

Adding and Subtracting Like Fractions

A **fraction** is a number that names part of a whole. Examples of fractions are $\frac{1}{2}$ and $\frac{1}{3}$. **Like fractions** have the same **denominator**, or bottom number. Examples of like fractions are $\frac{1}{4}$ and $\frac{3}{4}$.

To add or subtract fractions, the denominators must be the same. Add or subtract only the **numerators**, the numbers above the line in fractions.

Example:

numerators
denominators $\quad \frac{5}{8} - \frac{1}{8} = \frac{4}{8}$

$$\frac{5}{8} \qquad \frac{1}{8} \qquad \frac{4}{8}$$

Directions: Add or subtract these fractions.

$\frac{6}{12} - \frac{3}{12} =$	$\frac{4}{9} + \frac{1}{9} =$	$\frac{1}{3} + \frac{1}{3} =$	$\frac{5}{11} + \frac{4}{11} =$
$\frac{3}{5} - \frac{1}{5} =$	$\frac{5}{6} - \frac{2}{6} =$	$\frac{3}{4} - \frac{2}{4} =$	$\frac{5}{10} + \frac{3}{10} =$
$\frac{3}{8} + \frac{2}{8} =$	$\frac{1}{7} + \frac{4}{7} =$	$\frac{2}{20} + \frac{15}{20} =$	$\frac{11}{15} - \frac{9}{15} =$

Directions: Color the part of each pizza that equals the given fraction.

$$\frac{2}{4} \qquad + \qquad \frac{1}{4} \qquad =$$

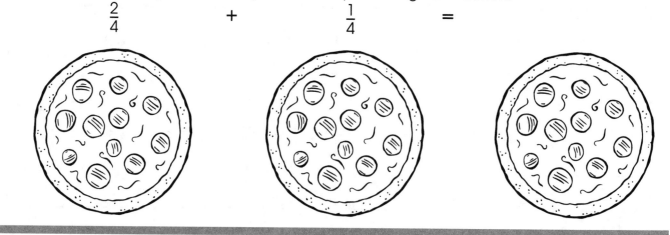

Name: _____

Adding and Subtracting Unlike Fractions

Unlike fractions have different denominators. Examples of unlike fractions are $\frac{1}{4}$ and $\frac{2}{5}$.
To add or subtract fractions, the denominators must be the same.

Example:

Step 1: Make the denominators the same by finding the least common denominator. The LCD of a pair of fractions is the same as the least common multiple (LCM) of their denominators.

$$\frac{1}{3} + \frac{1}{4} =$$

Multiples of 3 are 3, 6, 9, **12**, 15.
Multiples of 4 are 4, 8, **12**, 16.
LCM (and LCD) = 12

Step 2: Multiply by a number that will give the LCD. The numerator and denominator must be multiplied by the same number.

A. $\frac{1}{3} \times \frac{4}{4} = \frac{4}{12}$ **B.** $\frac{1}{4} \times \frac{3}{3} = \frac{3}{12}$

Step 3: Add the fractions. $\frac{1}{3} + \frac{1}{4} = \frac{4}{12} + \frac{3}{12} = \frac{7}{12}$

Directions: Follow the above steps to add or subtract unlike fractions. Write the LCM.

$\frac{2}{4} + \frac{3}{8} =$ LCM = _____	$\frac{3}{6} + \frac{1}{3} =$ LCM = _____	$\frac{4}{5} - \frac{1}{4} =$ LCM = _____
$\frac{2}{3} + \frac{2}{9} =$ LCM = _____	$\frac{4}{7} - \frac{2}{14} =$ LCM = _____	$\frac{7}{12} - \frac{2}{4} =$ LCM = _____

The basketball team ordered two pizzas.
They left $\frac{1}{3}$ of one and $\frac{1}{4}$ of the other.
How much pizza was left?

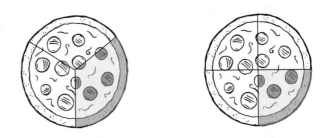

_____

Name: _____

Reducing Fractions

A fraction is in lowest terms when the GCF of both the numerator and denominator is 1. These fractions are in lowest possible terms: $\frac{2}{3}$, $\frac{5}{8}$ and $\frac{99}{100}$.

Example: Write $\frac{4}{8}$ in lowest terms.

Step 1: Write the factors of 4 and 8.

Factors of 4 are **4**, 2, 1.

Factors of 8 are 1, 8, 2, **4**.

Step 2: Find the GCF: 4.

Step 3: Divide both the numerator and denominator by 4.

Directions: Write each fraction in lowest terms.

$\frac{6}{8}$ = _____ lowest terms $\frac{9}{12}$ = _____ lowest terms

factors of 6: 6, 1, 2, 3   factors of 9: _____ , _____ , _____   _____ GCF

factors of 8: 8, 1, 2, 4   factors of 12: _____ , _____ , _____ , _____ , _____ , _____   _____ GCF

$\frac{2}{6}$ =	$\frac{10}{15}$ =	$\frac{8}{32}$ =	$\frac{4}{10}$ =
$\frac{12}{18}$ =	$\frac{6}{8}$ =	$\frac{4}{6}$ =	$\frac{3}{9}$ =

Directions: Color the pizzas to show that $\frac{4}{6}$ in lowest terms is $\frac{2}{3}$.

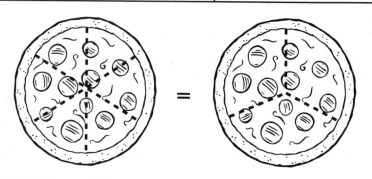

Adding and Subtracting Unlike Fractions

Directions: Find the LCD, then add or subtract. Reduce your answer to lowest terms by dividing both the numerator and denominator by the GCF.

$\frac{1}{3} - \frac{2}{9} =$

LCD = _____

GCF = _____

lowest terms _____

$\frac{5}{12} + \frac{1}{4} =$

LCD = _____

GCF = _____

lowest terms _____

$\frac{3}{8} + \frac{1}{2} =$

LCD = _____

GCF = _____

lowest terms _____

$\frac{2}{5} + \frac{1}{4} =$

LCD = _____

GCF = _____

lowest terms _____

$\frac{2}{3} - \frac{1}{6} =$

LCD = _____

GCF = _____

lowest terms _____

$\frac{3}{4} - \frac{5}{10} =$

LCD = _____

GCF = _____

lowest terms _____

$\frac{8}{12} - \frac{1}{3} =$

LCD = _____

GCF = _____

lowest terms _____

$\frac{8}{15} - \frac{1}{5} =$

LCD = _____

GCF = _____

lowest terms _____

$\frac{4}{7} - \frac{4}{14} =$

LCD = _____

GCF = _____

lowest terms _____

Joel and Jema competed in a bike race. After 30 minutes, Joel had finished $\frac{2}{3}$ of the race, and Jema had finished $\frac{7}{12}$ of the race. Who had finished more of the race?

_____

How much more of the race had that person finished?

_____

Improper Fractions

An **improper fraction** has a numerator that is greater than its denominator. An example of an improper fraction is $\frac{7}{6}$. An improper fraction should be reduced to its lowest terms.

Example: $\frac{5}{4}$ is an improper fraction because its numerator is greater than its denominator.

       Step 1: Divide the numerator by the denominator: $5 \div 4 = 1, \text{r}1$

       Step 2: Write the remainder as a fraction: $\frac{1}{4}$

       $\frac{5}{4} = 1\frac{1}{4}$ $1\frac{1}{4}$ is a mixed number—a whole number and a fraction.

Directions: Follow the steps above to change the improper fractions to mixed numbers.

$\frac{9}{8} =$	$\frac{11}{5} =$	$\frac{5}{3} =$	$\frac{7}{6} =$	$\frac{8}{7} =$	$\frac{4}{3} =$
$\frac{21}{5} =$	$\frac{9}{4} =$	$\frac{3}{2} =$	$\frac{9}{6} =$	$\frac{25}{4} =$	$\frac{8}{3} =$

Sara had 29 duplicate stamps in her stamp collection. She decided to give them to four of her friends. If she gave each of them the same number of stamps, how many duplicates will she have left? _____

Name the improper fraction in this problem. _____

What step must you do next to solve the problem? _____

_____

Write your answer as a mixed number. _____

How many stamps could she give each of her friends? _____

Name: _____

Mixed Numbers

A **mixed number** is a whole number and a fraction together. An example of a mixed number is $2\frac{3}{4}$. A mixed number can be changed to an improper fraction.

Example: $2\frac{3}{4}$

Step 1: Multiply the denominator by the whole number: $4 \times 2 = 8$

Step 2: Add the numerator: $8 + 3 = 11$

Step 3: Write the sum over the denominator: $\frac{11}{4}$

Directions: Follow the steps above to change the mixed numbers to improper fractions.

$3\frac{2}{3} =$	$6\frac{1}{5} =$	$4\frac{7}{8} =$	$2\frac{1}{2} =$
$1\frac{4}{5} =$	$5\frac{3}{4} =$	$7\frac{1}{8} =$	$9\frac{1}{9} =$
$8\frac{1}{2} =$	$7\frac{1}{6} =$	$5\frac{3}{5} =$	$9\frac{3}{8} =$
$12\frac{1}{5} =$	$25\frac{1}{2} =$	$10\frac{2}{3} =$	$14\frac{3}{8} =$

Name: _____

Improper Fractions and Mixed Numbers

Directions: Write the mixed number for each fraction. Reduce to lowest terms.

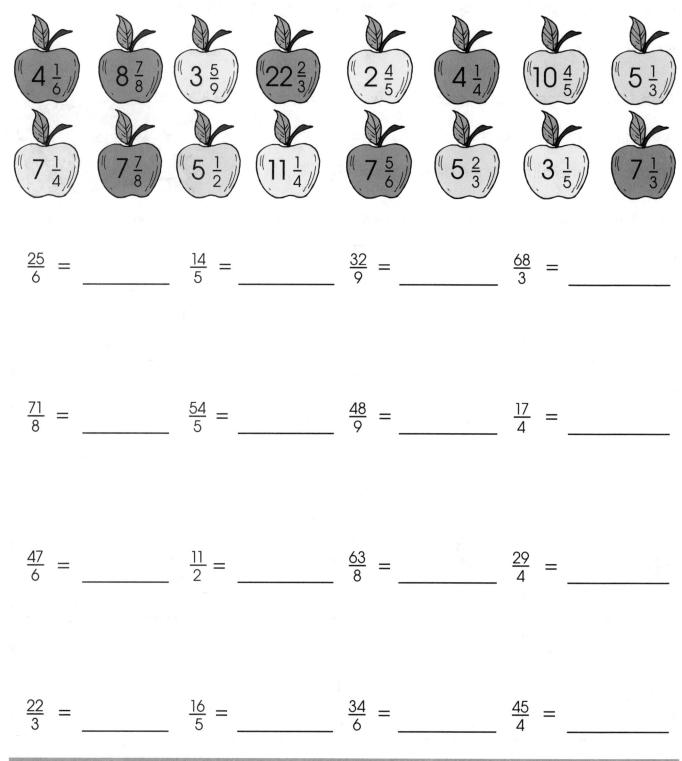

$\frac{25}{6}$ = _____

$\frac{14}{5}$ = _____

$\frac{32}{9}$ = _____

$\frac{68}{3}$ = _____

$\frac{71}{8}$ = _____

$\frac{54}{5}$ = _____

$\frac{48}{9}$ = _____

$\frac{17}{4}$ = _____

$\frac{47}{6}$ = _____

$\frac{11}{2}$ = _____

$\frac{63}{8}$ = _____

$\frac{29}{4}$ = _____

$\frac{22}{3}$ = _____

$\frac{16}{5}$ = _____

$\frac{34}{6}$ = _____

$\frac{45}{4}$ = _____

Name: _____

Adding Mixed Numbers

To add mixed numbers, first find the least common denominator.

Always reduce the answer to lowest terms.

Example:

$$5 \frac{1}{4} \longrightarrow 5 \frac{3}{12}$$

$$+ 6 \frac{1}{3} \longrightarrow + 6 \frac{4}{12}$$

$$11 \frac{7}{12}$$

Directions: Add. Reduce the answers to lowest terms.

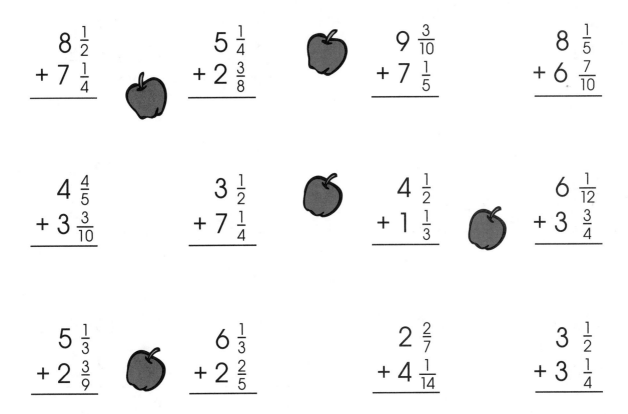

$$\begin{array}{r} 8 \frac{1}{2} \\ + 7 \frac{1}{4} \\ \hline \end{array}$$

$$\begin{array}{r} 5 \frac{1}{4} \\ + 2 \frac{3}{8} \\ \hline \end{array}$$

$$\begin{array}{r} 9 \frac{3}{10} \\ + 7 \frac{1}{5} \\ \hline \end{array}$$

$$\begin{array}{r} 8 \frac{1}{5} \\ + 6 \frac{7}{10} \\ \hline \end{array}$$

$$\begin{array}{r} 4 \frac{4}{5} \\ + 3 \frac{3}{10} \\ \hline \end{array}$$

$$\begin{array}{r} 3 \frac{1}{2} \\ + 7 \frac{1}{4} \\ \hline \end{array}$$

$$\begin{array}{r} 4 \frac{1}{2} \\ + 1 \frac{1}{3} \\ \hline \end{array}$$

$$\begin{array}{r} 6 \frac{1}{12} \\ + 3 \frac{3}{4} \\ \hline \end{array}$$

$$\begin{array}{r} 5 \frac{1}{3} \\ + 2 \frac{3}{9} \\ \hline \end{array}$$

$$\begin{array}{r} 6 \frac{1}{3} \\ + 2 \frac{2}{5} \\ \hline \end{array}$$

$$\begin{array}{r} 2 \frac{2}{7} \\ + 4 \frac{1}{14} \\ \hline \end{array}$$

$$\begin{array}{r} 3 \frac{1}{2} \\ + 3 \frac{1}{4} \\ \hline \end{array}$$

The boys picked $3\frac{1}{2}$ baskets of apples. The girls picked $5\frac{1}{2}$ baskets. How many baskets of apples did the boys and girls pick in all?

_____

Name: _____

Subtracting Mixed Numbers

To subtract mixed numbers, first find the least common denominator. Reduce the answer to its lowest terms.

Directions: Subtract. Reduce to lowest terms.

Example:

$$6 \frac{5}{8} \rightarrow 6 \frac{10}{16}$$
$$- 3 \frac{4}{16} \rightarrow - 3 \frac{4}{16}$$
$$\overline{ 3 \frac{6}{16} = 3 \frac{3}{8}}$$

$$2 \frac{3}{7}$$
$$- 1 \frac{1}{14}$$

$$7 \frac{2}{3}$$
$$- 5 \frac{1}{8}$$

$$6 \frac{3}{4}$$
$$- 2 \frac{3}{12}$$

$$9 \frac{5}{12}$$
$$- 5 \frac{9}{24}$$

$$5 \frac{1}{2}$$
$$- 3 \frac{1}{3}$$

$$7 \frac{3}{8}$$
$$- 5 \frac{1}{6}$$

$$8 \frac{3}{8}$$
$$- 6 \frac{5}{12}$$

$$11 \frac{5}{6}$$
$$- 7 \frac{1}{12}$$

$$9 \frac{3}{5}$$
$$- 7 \frac{1}{15}$$

$$4 \frac{4}{5}$$
$$- 2 \frac{1}{4}$$

$$9 \frac{2}{3}$$
$$- 4 \frac{1}{6}$$

$$14 \frac{3}{8}$$
$$- 9 \frac{3}{16}$$

The Rodriguez Farm has $9\frac{1}{2}$ acres of corn. The Johnson Farm has $7\frac{1}{3}$ acres of corn. How many more acres of corn does the Rodriguez Farm have? _____

Name: _____

Review

Directions: Match.

$\frac{1}{4}$ + $\frac{1}{3}$ $\frac{19}{8}$

$\frac{1}{5}$ − $\frac{1}{6}$ $\frac{7}{5}$

1 $\frac{1}{6}$ $\frac{1}{30}$

1 $\frac{2}{5}$ $\frac{7}{12}$

2 $\frac{3}{8}$ $\frac{7}{6}$

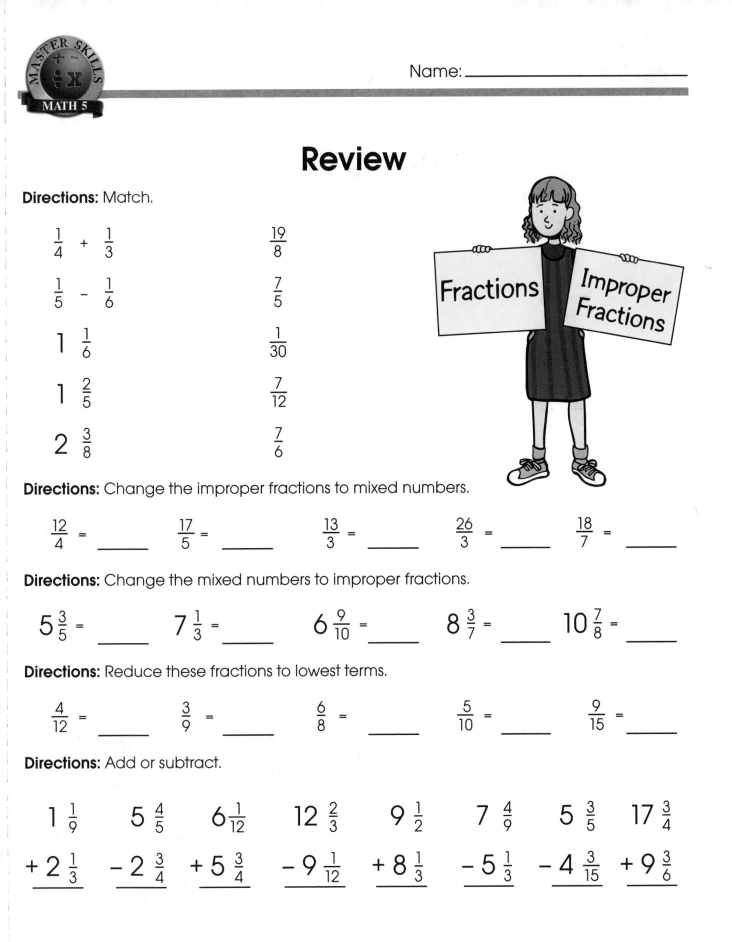

Directions: Change the improper fractions to mixed numbers.

$\frac{12}{4}$ = _____ $\frac{17}{5}$ = _____ $\frac{13}{3}$ = _____ $\frac{26}{3}$ = _____ $\frac{18}{7}$ = _____

Directions: Change the mixed numbers to improper fractions.

$5\frac{3}{5}$ = _____ $7\frac{1}{3}$ = _____ $6\frac{9}{10}$ = _____ $8\frac{3}{7}$ = _____ $10\frac{7}{8}$ = _____

Directions: Reduce these fractions to lowest terms.

$\frac{4}{12}$ = _____ $\frac{3}{9}$ = _____ $\frac{6}{8}$ = _____ $\frac{5}{10}$ = _____ $\frac{9}{15}$ = _____

Directions: Add or subtract.

$1\frac{1}{9}$ $5\frac{4}{5}$ $6\frac{1}{12}$ $12\frac{2}{3}$ $9\frac{1}{2}$ $7\frac{4}{9}$ $5\frac{3}{5}$ $17\frac{3}{4}$

$+2\frac{1}{3}$ $-2\frac{3}{4}$ $+5\frac{3}{4}$ $-9\frac{1}{12}$ $+8\frac{1}{3}$ $-5\frac{1}{3}$ $-4\frac{3}{15}$ $+9\frac{3}{6}$

Name: _____

Comparing Fractions

Directions: Use the symbol **>** (greater than), **<** (less than) or **=** (equal to) to show the relationship between each pair of fractions.

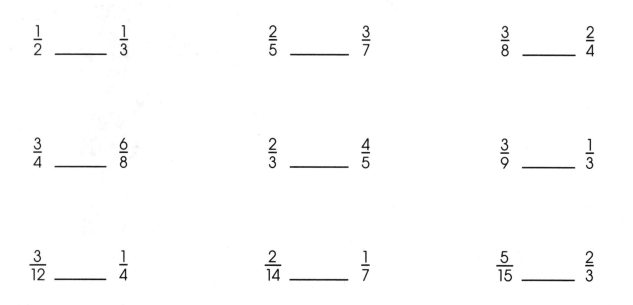

$\dfrac{1}{2}$ _____ $\dfrac{1}{3}$ $\qquad$ $\dfrac{2}{5}$ _____ $\dfrac{3}{7}$ $\qquad$ $\dfrac{3}{8}$ _____ $\dfrac{2}{4}$

$\dfrac{3}{4}$ _____ $\dfrac{6}{8}$ $\qquad$ $\dfrac{2}{3}$ _____ $\dfrac{4}{5}$ $\qquad$ $\dfrac{3}{9}$ _____ $\dfrac{1}{3}$

$\dfrac{3}{12}$ _____ $\dfrac{1}{4}$ $\qquad$ $\dfrac{2}{14}$ _____ $\dfrac{1}{7}$ $\qquad$ $\dfrac{5}{15}$ _____ $\dfrac{2}{3}$

If Kelly gave $\dfrac{1}{3}$ of a pizza to Holly and $\dfrac{1}{5}$ to Diane, how much did she have left?

_____

Holly decided to share $\dfrac{1}{2}$ of her share of the pizza with Deb. How much did each of them actually get?

_____

Name: _____

Ordering Fractions

When putting fractions in order from smallest to largest or largest to smallest, it helps to find a common denominator first.

Example:

$$\frac{1}{3} \; , \; \frac{1}{2} \qquad \text{changed to} \qquad \frac{2}{6} \; , \; \frac{3}{6}$$

Directions: Put the following fractions in order from least to largest value.

				Least			Largest
$\frac{1}{2}$	$\frac{2}{7}$	$\frac{4}{5}$	$\frac{1}{3}$	_____	_____	_____	_____
$\frac{3}{12}$	$\frac{3}{6}$	$\frac{1}{3}$	$\frac{3}{4}$	_____	_____	_____	_____
$\frac{2}{5}$	$\frac{4}{15}$	$\frac{3}{5}$	$\frac{5}{15}$	_____	_____	_____	_____
$3\frac{4}{5}$	$3\frac{2}{5}$	$\frac{9}{5}$	$3\frac{1}{5}$	_____	_____	_____	_____
$9\frac{1}{3}$	$9\frac{2}{3}$	$9\frac{9}{12}$	$8\frac{2}{3}$	_____	_____	_____	_____
$5\frac{8}{12}$	$5\frac{5}{12}$	$5\frac{4}{24}$	$5\frac{3}{6}$	_____	_____	_____	_____
$4\frac{3}{5}$	$5\frac{7}{15}$	$6\frac{2}{5}$	$5\frac{1}{5}$	_____	_____	_____	_____

Four dogs were selected as finalists at a dog show. They were judged in four separate categories. One received a perfect score in each area. The dog with a score closest to four is the winner. Their scores are listed below. Which dog won the contest? _____

Dog A	$3\frac{4}{5}$	Dog B	$3\frac{2}{3}$	Dog C	$3\frac{5}{15}$	Dog D	$3\frac{9}{12}$

Name: _____

Multiplying Fractions

To multiply fractions, follow these steps:

$\frac{1}{2} \times \frac{3}{4} =$ **Step 1:** Multiply the numerators. $1 \times 3 = \frac{3}{8}$
Step 2: Multiply the denominators. $2 \times 4 = 8$

When multiplying a fraction by a whole number, first change the whole number to a fraction.

Example:

$\frac{1}{2} \times 8 = \frac{1}{2} \times \frac{8}{1} = \frac{8}{2} = 4$ reduced to lowest terms

Directions: Multiply. Reduce your answers to lowest terms.

$\frac{3}{4} \times \frac{1}{6} =$	$\frac{1}{2} \times \frac{5}{8} =$	$\frac{2}{3} \times \frac{1}{6} =$	$\frac{2}{3} \times \frac{1}{2} =$
$\frac{5}{6} \times 4 =$	$\frac{3}{8} \times \frac{1}{16} =$	$\frac{1}{5} \times 5 =$	$\frac{7}{8} \times \frac{3}{4} =$
$\frac{7}{11} \times \frac{1}{3} =$	$\frac{2}{9} \times \frac{9}{4} =$	$\frac{1}{3} \times \frac{1}{3} \times \frac{1}{3} =$	$\frac{1}{8} \times \frac{1}{4} \times \frac{1}{2} =$

Jennifer has 10 pets. Two-fifths of the pets are cats, one-half are fish and one-tenth are dogs. How many of each pet does she have?

_____
_____
_____

Multiplying Mixed Numbers

Multiply mixed numbers by first changing them to improper fractions. Always reduce your answers to lowest terms.

Example:

$$2\frac{1}{3} \times 1\frac{1}{8} = \frac{7}{3} \times \frac{9}{8} = \frac{63}{24} = 2\frac{15}{24} = 2\frac{5}{8}$$

Directions: Multiply. Reduce to lowest terms.

$4\frac{1}{4} \times 2\frac{1}{5} =$	$1\frac{1}{3} \times 3\frac{1}{4} =$	$1\frac{1}{9} \times 3\frac{3}{5} =$
$1\frac{6}{7} \times 4\frac{1}{2} =$	$2\frac{3}{4} \times 2\frac{3}{5} =$	$4\frac{2}{3} \times 3\frac{1}{7} =$
$6\frac{2}{5} \times 2\frac{1}{8} =$	$3\frac{1}{7} \times 4\frac{5}{8} =$	$7\frac{3}{8} \times 2\frac{1}{9} =$

Sunnyside Farm has two barns with 25 stalls in each barn.
Cows use $\frac{3}{5}$ of the stalls, and horses use the rest.

How many stalls are for cows? _____

How many are for horses? _____

(Hint: First, find how many total stalls are in the two barns.)

Name: _____

Dividing Fractions

To divide fractions, follow these steps:

$$\frac{3}{4} \div \frac{1}{4} =$$

Step 1: "Invert" the divisor. That means to turn it upside down.

$$\frac{3}{4} \div \frac{4}{1}$$

Step 2: Multiply the two fractions:

$$\frac{3}{4} \times \frac{4}{1} = \frac{12}{4}$$

Step 3: Reduce the fraction to lowest terms by dividing the denominator into the numerator.

$$12 \div 4 = 3$$

$$\frac{3}{4} \div \frac{1}{4} = 3$$

Directions: Follow the above steps to divide fractions.

$\frac{1}{4} \div \frac{1}{5} =$	$\frac{1}{3} \div \frac{1}{12} =$	$\frac{3}{4} \div \frac{1}{3} =$
$\frac{5}{12} \div \frac{1}{3} =$	$\frac{3}{4} \div \frac{1}{6} =$	$\frac{2}{9} \div \frac{2}{3} =$
$\frac{3}{7} \div \frac{1}{4} =$	$\frac{2}{3} \div \frac{4}{6} =$	$\frac{1}{8} \div \frac{2}{3} =$
$\frac{4}{5} \div \frac{1}{3} =$	$\frac{4}{8} \div \frac{1}{2} =$	$\frac{5}{12} \div \frac{6}{8} =$

Name: _____

Dividing Whole Numbers by Fractions

Follow these steps to divide a whole number by a fraction:

$$8 \div \frac{1}{4} =$$

Step 1: Write the whole number as a fraction:

$$\frac{8}{1} \div \frac{1}{4} =$$

Step 2: Invert the divisor.

$$\frac{8}{1} \div \frac{4}{1} =$$

Step 3: Multiply the two fractions:

$$\frac{8}{1} \times \frac{4}{1} = \frac{32}{1}$$

Step 4: Reduce the fraction to lowest terms by dividing the denominator into the numerator: $32 \div 1 = 32$

Directions: Follow the above steps to divide a whole number by a fraction.

$6 \div \frac{1}{3} =$	$4 \div \frac{1}{2} =$	$21 \div \frac{1}{3} =$
$8 \div \frac{1}{2} =$	$3 \div \frac{1}{6} =$	$15 \div \frac{1}{7} =$
$9 \div \frac{1}{5} =$	$4 \div \frac{1}{9} =$	$12 \div \frac{1}{6} =$

Three-fourths of a bag of popcorn fits into one bowl.
How many bowls do you need if you have six bags of popcorn? _____

Name: _____

Division Word Problems

Directions: Divide.

Brian has 2,000 small building blocks. He decided to share them with his cousin, Tina. He gave Tina one-fourth of the blocks. How many blocks did he keep?

_____

Tim has a collection of toy cars. His mother asked him to give one-third of them to his sister, Tori. He gave Tori 135 cars. How many did he keep for himself?

_____

How many did he have before giving some of them away?

_____

Becky ordered two extra large pizzas for her four children. Each of the pizzas had been cut into 16 slices. If the children have equal servings, what fraction of the pizzas will each child get?

_____

How many slices of pizza would that equal?

_____

It normally takes Joel 1 hour to mow the yard. Today he only completed four-fifths of the job. How long did he work?

_____

If it takes Kristen 20 minutes to do one-fifth of her homework, how long will it take her to do one-half of it?

_____

Name: _____

Decimals

A **decimal** is a number with one or more places to the right of a decimal point.

Examples: 6.5 and 2.25

Fractions with denominators of 10 or 100 can be written as decimals.

1/2   0.50

Examples:

$\frac{7}{10}$ = 0.7

$$\frac{0}{\text{ones}} \cdot \frac{7}{\text{tenths}} \quad \frac{0}{\text{hundredths}}$$

$1\frac{52}{100}$ = 1.52

$$\frac{1}{\text{ones}} \cdot \frac{5}{\text{tenths}} \quad \frac{2}{\text{hundredths}}$$

Directions: Write the fractions as decimals.

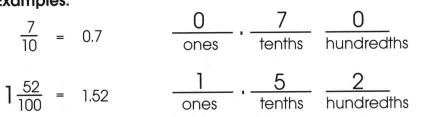

$\frac{1}{2}$ = $\overline{10}$ = 0. _____

$\frac{2}{5}$ = $\overline{10}$ = 0. _____

$\frac{1}{5}$ = $\overline{10}$ = 0. _____

$\frac{3}{5}$ = $\overline{10}$ = 0. _____

			1/10
	$\frac{1}{4}$	$\frac{1}{5}$	1/10
$\frac{1}{2}$			1/10
	$\frac{1}{4}$	$\frac{1}{5}$	1/10
		$\frac{1}{5}$	1/10
	$\frac{1}{4}$		1/10
$\frac{1}{2}$		$\frac{1}{5}$	1/10
	$\frac{1}{4}$	$\frac{1}{5}$	1/10
			1/10

$\frac{63}{100}$ =	$2\frac{8}{10}$ =	$38\frac{4}{100}$ =	$6\frac{13}{100}$ =
$\frac{1}{4}$ =	$\frac{2}{5}$ =	$\frac{1}{50}$ =	$\frac{100}{200}$ =
$5\frac{2}{100}$ =	$\frac{4}{25}$ =	$15\frac{3}{5}$ =	$\frac{3}{100}$ =

Name: _____

Decimals and Fractions

Directions: Write the letter of the fraction that is equal to the decimal.

0.25 = _____

0.5 = _____

0.7 = _____

0.8 = _____

0.37 = _____

0.2 = _____

0.65 = _____

0.75 = _____

0.6 = _____

0.12 = _____

0.33 = _____

0.95 = _____

0.24 = _____

0.3 = _____

0.4 = _____

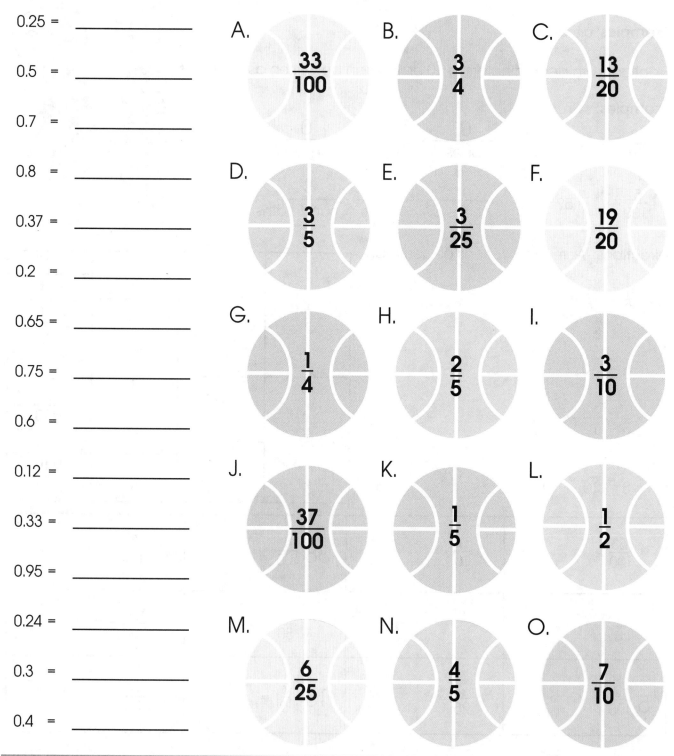

A. $\dfrac{33}{100}$

B. $\dfrac{3}{4}$

C. $\dfrac{13}{20}$

D. $\dfrac{3}{5}$

E. $\dfrac{3}{25}$

F. $\dfrac{19}{20}$

G. $\dfrac{1}{4}$

H. $\dfrac{2}{5}$

I. $\dfrac{3}{10}$

J. $\dfrac{37}{100}$

K. $\dfrac{1}{5}$

L. $\dfrac{1}{2}$

M. $\dfrac{6}{25}$

N. $\dfrac{4}{5}$

O. $\dfrac{7}{10}$

Name: _____

Adding and Subtracting Decimals

A decimal is another way of writing a fraction. Decimals and fractions are numbers less than one.

Directions: Add or subtract. Remember to keep the decimal point in the proper place.

$$
\begin{array}{r} 0.5 \\ + 0.8 \\ \hline \end{array} \quad 0.13
$$

$$
\begin{array}{r} 0.35 \\ + 0.25 \\ \hline \end{array} \quad 0.60
$$

$$
\begin{array}{r} 47.5 \\ - 32.7 \\ \hline \end{array}
$$

$$
\begin{array}{r} 85.7 \\ - 9.8 \\ \hline \end{array}
$$

$$
\begin{array}{r} 13.90 \\ + 4.23 \\ \hline \end{array} \quad 17.113
$$

$$
\begin{array}{r} 9.53 \\ - 8.16 \\ \hline \end{array}
$$

$$
\begin{array}{r} 72.8 \\ - 63.9 \\ \hline \end{array}
$$

$$
\begin{array}{r} 6.43 \\ + 4.58 \\ \hline \end{array} \quad 10.111
$$

$$
\begin{array}{r} 638.07 \\ - 19.34 \\ \hline \end{array}
$$

$$
\begin{array}{r} 811.060 \\ + 78.430 \\ \hline \end{array} \quad 889490
$$

$$
\begin{array}{r} 521.09 \\ - 148.75 \\ \hline \end{array}
$$

$$
\begin{array}{r} 916.635 \\ + 172.136 \\ \hline \end{array} \quad 1088.771
$$

$$
\begin{array}{r} 287.768 \\ - 63.951 \\ \hline \end{array}
$$

$$
\begin{array}{r} 467.05 \\ - 398.19 \\ \hline \end{array}
$$

Sean ran a 1-mile race in 5.58 minutes. Carlos ran it in 6.38 minutes. How much faster did Sean run?

_____

Name: _____

Multiplying Decimals

Multiply with decimals the same way you do with whole numbers. The decimal point moves in multiplication. Count the number of decimals in the problem and use the same number of decimals in your answer.

Example:

```
   3.5
 x 1.5
  175
  35
 5.25
```

Directions: Multiply.

2.5	67.4	83.7	13.35
x .9	x 2.3	x 9.8	x 3.06

9.06	28.97	33.41	28.7
x 2.38	x 5.16	x .93	x 11.9

The jet flies 1.5 times faster than the plane with a propeller. The propeller plane flies 165.7 miles per hour. How fast does the jet fly?

_____

Dividing With Decimals

When the dividend has a decimal, place the decimal point for the answer directly above the decimal point in the dividend. The first one has been done for you.

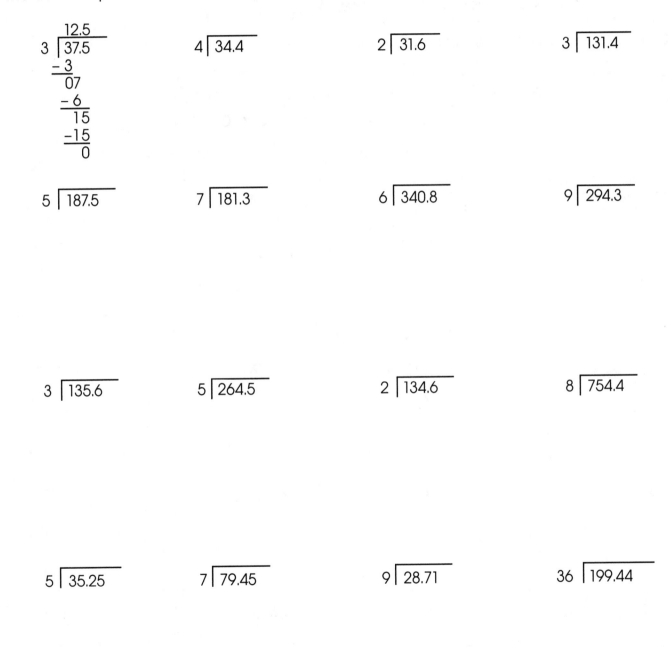

$$
\begin{array}{r}
12.5 \\
3\overline{)37.5} \\
\underline{-3} \\
07 \\
\underline{-6} \\
15 \\
\underline{-15} \\
0
\end{array}
$$

$4\overline{)34.4}$ $2\overline{)31.6}$ $3\overline{)131.4}$

$5\overline{)187.5}$ $7\overline{)181.3}$ $6\overline{)340.8}$ $9\overline{)294.3}$

$3\overline{)135.6}$ $5\overline{)264.5}$ $2\overline{)134.6}$ $8\overline{)754.4}$

$5\overline{)35.25}$ $7\overline{)79.45}$ $9\overline{)28.71}$ $36\overline{)199.44}$

Name: _____

Dividing Decimals by Decimals

When the divisor has a decimal, you must eliminate it before dividing. You can do this by moving it to the right to create a whole number. You must also move the decimal the same number of spaces to the right in the dividend.

Sometimes you need to add zeros to do this.

Example:

$$0.25\overline{)85.50}$$ changes to
$$\begin{array}{r} 342 \\ 25\overline{)8550} \\ -75 \\ \hline 105 \\ -100 \\ \hline 50 \\ 50 \\ \hline 0 \end{array}$$

Directions: Divide.

$$0.3\overline{)27.9}$$ $$0.6\overline{)42.6}$$ $$0.9\overline{)81.9}$$ $$0.7\overline{)83.3}$$

$$0.4\overline{)23.2}$$ $$0.7\overline{)56.7}$$ $$1.2\overline{)10.8}$$ $$2.2\overline{)138.6}$$

$$12.6\overline{)5,670}$$ $$4.7\overline{)564}$$ $$8.6\overline{)842.8}$$ $$3.7\overline{)2,009.1}$$

$$5.9\overline{)1,917.5}$$ $$4.3\overline{)1,376}$$ $$2.9\overline{)922.2}$$ $$2.7\overline{)5613.3}$$

Name: _____

Review

Directions: Multiply. Reduce to lowest terms.

$\frac{1}{4}$ x $\frac{1}{5}$ =	$\frac{5}{8}$ x $\frac{3}{10}$ =	$\frac{2}{9}$ x $\frac{3}{4}$ =	$\frac{5}{12}$ x $\frac{8}{15}$ =
$5\frac{1}{4}$ x $3\frac{1}{5}$ =	$3\frac{3}{4}$ x $2\frac{1}{7}$ =	$4\frac{1}{6}$ x $3\frac{3}{5}$ =	$6\frac{3}{8}$ x $1\frac{1}{9}$ =

Directions: Divide. Reduce to lowest terms.

$5 \div \frac{1}{5}$ =	$18 \div \frac{1}{9}$ =	$8 \div \frac{1}{3}$ =
$18 \div \frac{1}{4}$ =	$63 \div \frac{5}{8}$ =	$42 \div \frac{1}{5}$ =

Directions: Write these fractions as decimals.

$\frac{7}{100}$ = _____ $\frac{2}{5}$ = _____ $37\frac{3}{10}$ = _____ $\frac{5}{100}$ = _____

Directions: Add or subtract.

$$\begin{array}{r} 14.5 \\ + \ 3.8 \\ \hline \end{array}$$
8.13

$$\begin{array}{r} 26.93 \\ - 18.45 \\ \hline \end{array}$$

$$\begin{array}{r} 137.092 \\ - \ 98.135 \\ \hline \end{array}$$

$$\begin{array}{r} 291.036 \\ + 187.984 \\ \hline \end{array}$$
478.1020

Directions: Multiply.

$$\begin{array}{r} 83.3 \\ \times \ 0.6 \\ \hline \end{array}$$

$$\begin{array}{r} 42.91 \\ \times \ 2.03 \\ \hline \end{array}$$

$$\begin{array}{r} 12.3 \\ \times \ 0.7 \\ \hline \end{array}$$

$$\begin{array}{r} 27.09 \\ \times \ 3.16 \\ \hline \end{array}$$

Name: _____

Geometry

Geometry is the branch of mathematics that has to do with points, lines and shapes.

Directions: Use the Glossary on pages 105 and 106 if you need help. Write the word from the box that is described below.

triangle	square	cube	angle
line	ray	segment	rectangle

a collection of points on a straight path
that goes on and on in opposite directions _____

a figure with three sides and three corners _____

a figure with four equal sides
and four corners _____

part of a line that has one end point
and goes on and on in one direction _____

part of a line having two end points _____

a space figure with six square faces _____

two rays with a common end point _____

a figure with four corners and four sides _____

Name: _____

Geometry

Review the definitions on the previous page before completing the problems below.

Directions: Identify the labeled section of each of the following diagrams.

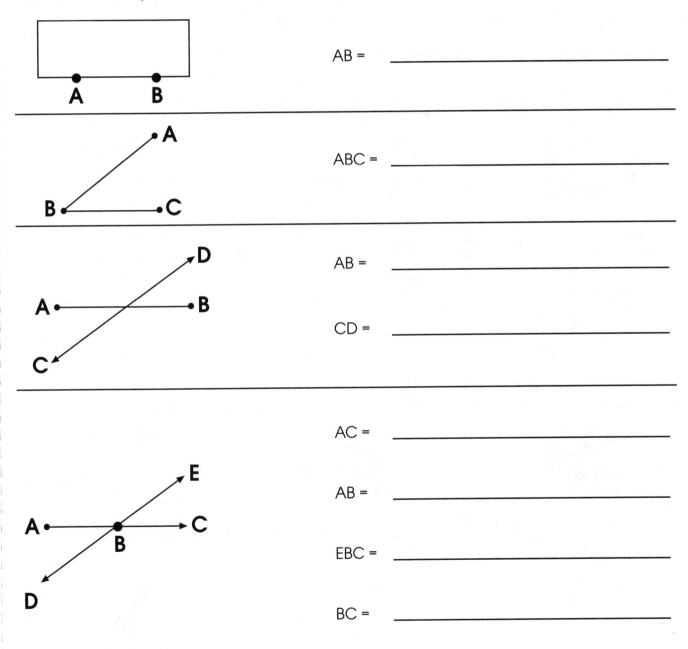

AB = _____

ABC = _____

AB = _____

CD = _____

AC = _____

AB = _____

EBC = _____

BC = _____

Name: _____

Similar, Congruent and Symmetrical Figures

Similar figures have the same shape but have varying sizes.

Figures that are **congruent** have identical shapes but different orientations. That means they face in different directions.

Symmetrical figures can be divided equally into two identical parts.

Directions: Cross out the shape that does not belong in each group. Label the two remaining shapes as similiar, congruent or symmetrical.

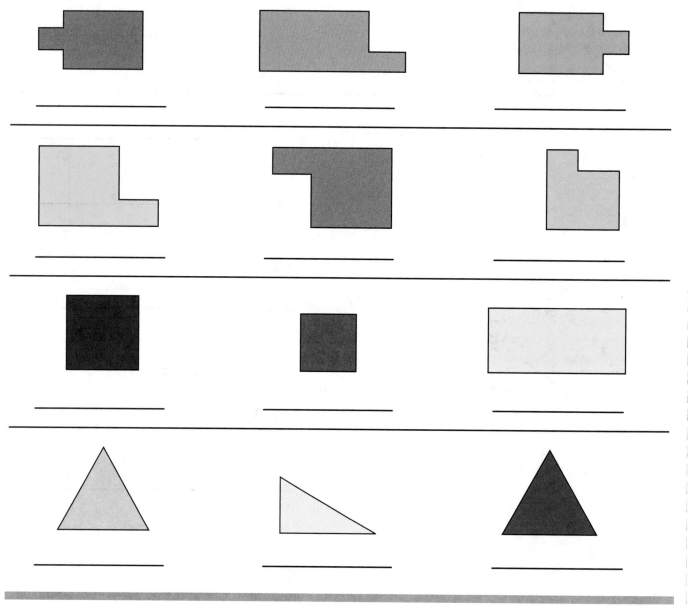

Name: _____

Perimeter and Area

The **perimeter (P)** of a figure is the distance around it. To find the perimeter, add the lengths of the sides.

The **area (A)** of a figure is the number of units in a figure. Find the area by multiplying the length of a figure by its width.

Example:

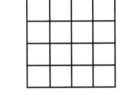

P = 16 units
A = 16 units

Directions: Find the perimeter and area of each figure.

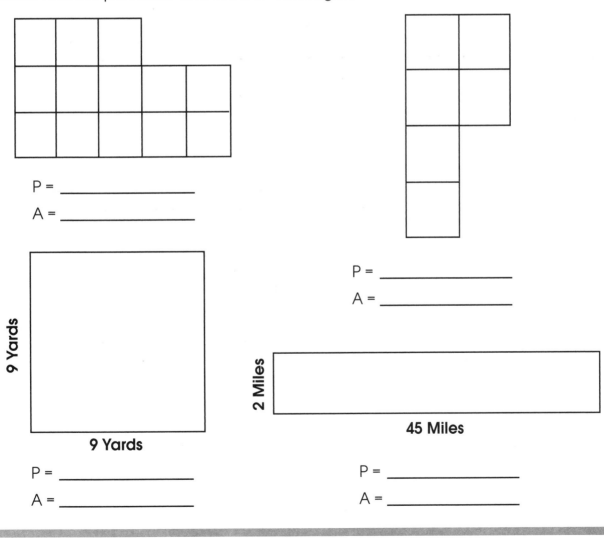

P = _____

A = _____

P = _____

A = _____

9 Yards

9 Yards

P = _____

A = _____

2 Miles

45 Miles

P = _____

A = _____

Volume

The **volume** of a figure is the number of cubic units inside it.

Example: Volume = 6 cubic units

Directions: Draw figures to show the volumes given. Use the dot pattern to help you. The first one has been done for you.

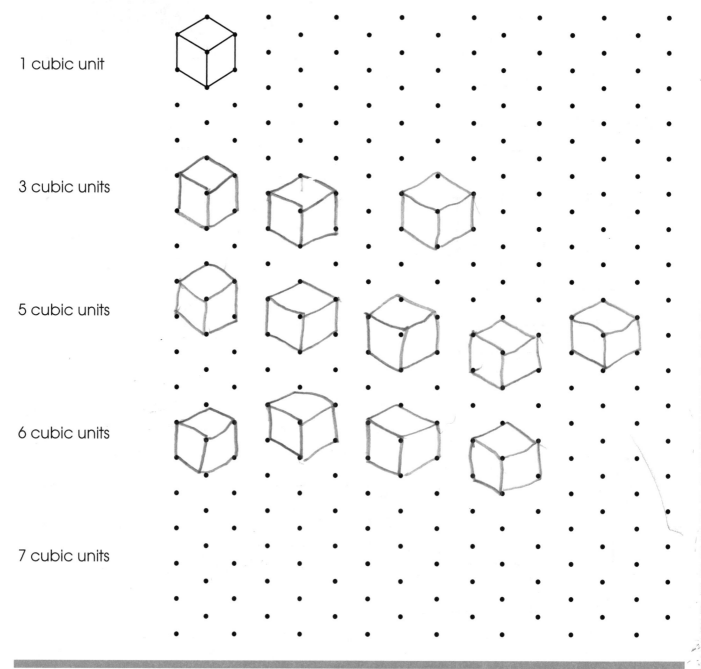

1 cubic unit

3 cubic units

5 cubic units

6 cubic units

7 cubic units

Name: _____

Volume

The formula for finding the volume of a box is length times width times height **(L x W x H)**. The answer is given in cubic units.

Directions: Solve the problems.

Example:

Height 8 ft.
Length 8 ft.
Width   8 ft. **L** x **W** x **H** = **volume**
8' x 8' x 8' = 512 cubic ft. or 512 ft.^{3}

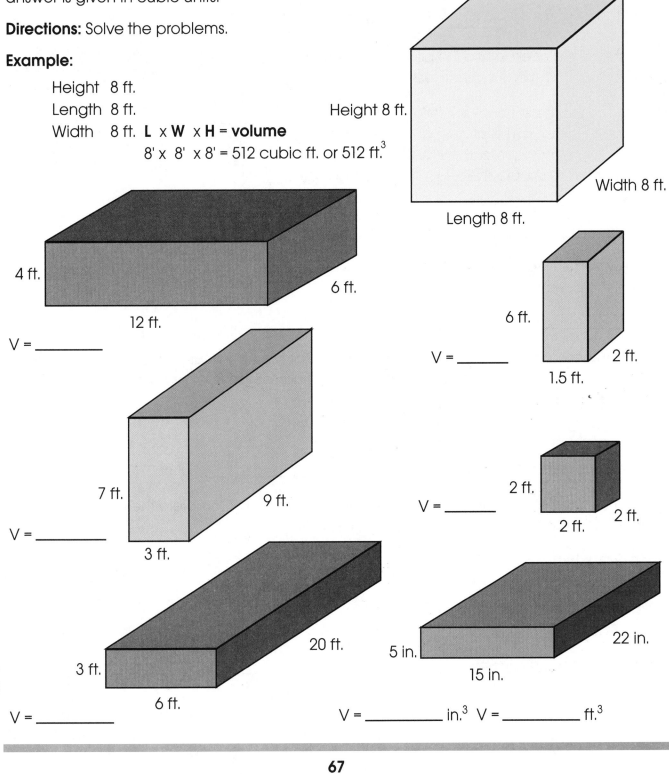

Height 8 ft.

Width 8 ft.

Length 8 ft.

4 ft.

6 ft.

12 ft.

V = _____

7 ft.

9 ft.

3 ft.

V = _____

6 ft.

2 ft.

1.5 ft.

V = _____

2 ft.

2 ft.

2 ft.

V = _____

20 ft.

3 ft.

6 ft.

V = _____

5 in.

22 in.

15 in.

V = _____ in.^{3} V = _____ ft.^{3}

Name: _____

Perimeter and Area

Directions: Use the formulas for finding perimeter and area to solve these problems.

Julie's family moved to a new house. Her parents said she could have the largest bedroom. Julie knew she would need to find the perimeter of each room to find which one was largest.

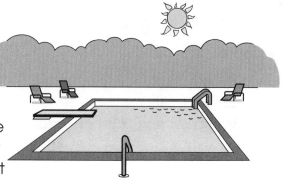

One rectangular bedroom is 7 feet wide and 12 feet long. Another is 11 feet long and 9 feet wide. The third bedroom is a square. It is 9 feet wide and 9 feet long. Which one should she select to have the largest room?

_____

The new home also has a swimming pool in the backyard. It is 32 feet long and 18 feet wide. What is the perimeter of the pool?

_____

Julie's mother wants to plant flowers on each side of the new house. She will need three plants for every foot of space. The house is 75 feet across the front and back and 37.5 feet along each side. Find the perimeter of the house.

_____

How many plants should she buy? _____

The family decided to buy new carpeting for several rooms. Complete the necessary information to determine how much carpeting to buy.

Den: 12 ft. x 14 ft. = _____ sq. ft.

Master Bedroom: 20 ft. x _____ = 360 sq. ft.

Family Room: _____ x 25 ft. = 375 sq. ft.

Total square feet of carpeting: _____

Name: _____

Perimeter and Area

Directions: Find the perimeter and area.

1. Length = 8 ft.

   Width = 11 ft.

   P = _____ A = _____

2. Length = 12 ft.

   Width = 10 ft.

   P = _____ A = _____

3. Length = 121 ft.

   Width = 16 ft.

   P = _____ A = _____

4. Length = 72 in.

   Width = 5 ft.

   P = _____ A = _____

Directions: Find the perimeter, area and volume.

5. Length = 7 ft.

   Width = 12 ft.

   Height = 10 ft.

   P = _____

   A = _____

   V = _____

6. Length = 48 in.

   Width = 7 ft.

   Height = 12 in.

   P = _____

   A = _____

   V = _____

7. Length = 12 in.

   Width = 15 in.

   Height = 20 in.

   P = _____

   A = _____

   V = _____

8. Length = 22 ft.

   Width = 40 ft.

   Height = 10 ft.

   P = _____

   A = _____

   V = _____

Name: _____

Circumference

Circumference is the distance around a circle. The **diameter** is a line segment that passes through the center of a circle and has both end points on the circle.

To find the circumference of any circle, multiply 3.14 times the diameter. The number 3.14 represents **pi** (pronounced *pie*) and is often written by this Greek symbol, π.

The formula for circumference is C = π x d

    C = circumference

    d = diameter

    π = 3.14

Example:

    Circle A
    d = 2 in.
    C = 3.14 x 2 in.
    C = 6.28 in.

Directions: Find the circumference of each circle.

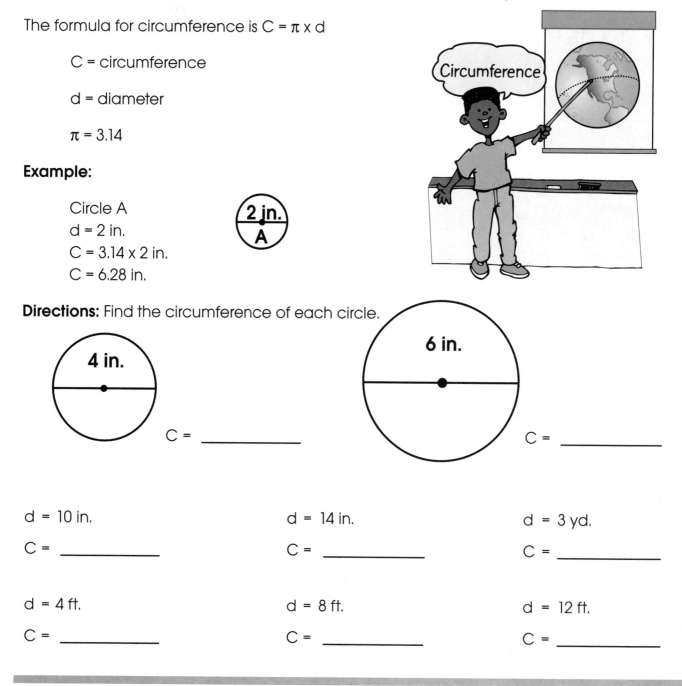

C = _____

C = _____

d = 10 in.	d = 14 in.	d = 3 yd.
C = _____	C = _____	C = _____

d = 4 ft.	d = 8 ft.	d = 12 ft.
C = _____	C = _____	C = _____

Name: _____

Circumference

The **radius** of a circle is the distance from the center of the circle to its outside edge. The diameter equals two times the radius.

Find the circumference by multiplying π (3.14) times the diameter or by multiplying π (3.14) times 2r (2 times the radius).

C = π x d or C = π x 2r

Directions: Write the missing radius, diameter or circumference.

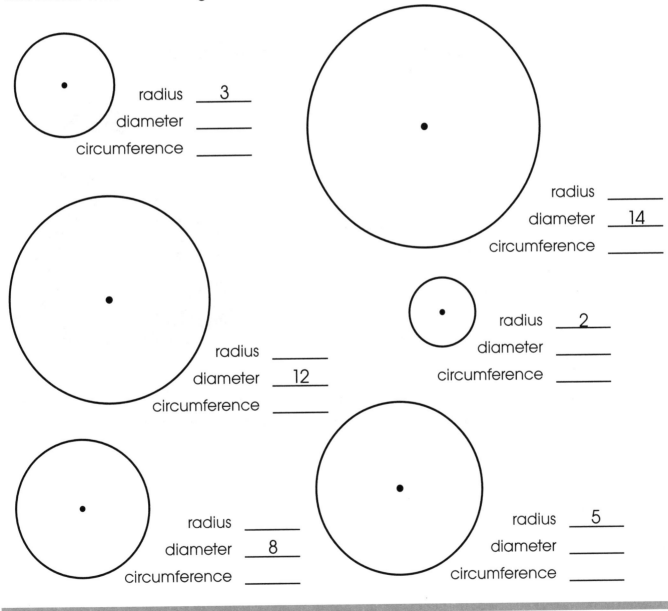

radius ___3___
diameter _____
circumference _____

radius _____
diameter ___14___
circumference _____

radius _____
diameter ___12___
circumference _____

radius ___2___
diameter _____
circumference _____

radius _____
diameter ___8___
circumference _____

radius ___5___
diameter _____
circumference _____

Diameter, Radius and Circumference

$C = \pi \times d$ or $C = \pi \times 2r$

Directions: Write the missing radius, diameter or circumference.

Katie was asked to draw a circle on the playground for a game during recess. If the radius of the circle needed to be 14 inches, how long is the diameter? _____

What is the circumference? _____

A friend told her that more kids could play the game if they enlarged the circle. She had a friend help her. They made the diameter of the circle 45 inches long.

What is the radius? _____

What is the circumference? _____

Jamie was creating an art project. He wanted part of it to be a sphere. He measured 24 inches for the diameter.

What would the radius of the sphere be? _____

Find the circumference. _____

Unfortunately, Jamie discovered that he didn't have enough material to create a sphere that large, so he cut the dimensions in half. What are the new dimensions for his sphere?

Radius _____

Diameter _____

Circumference _____

Name: _____

Triangle Angles

A **triangle** is a figure with three corners and three sides. Every triangle contains three angles. The sum of the angles is always 180°, regardless of the size or shape of the triangle.

If you know two of the angles, you can add them together, then subtract the total from 180 to find the number of degrees in the third angle.

Directions: Find the number of degrees in the third angle of each triangle.

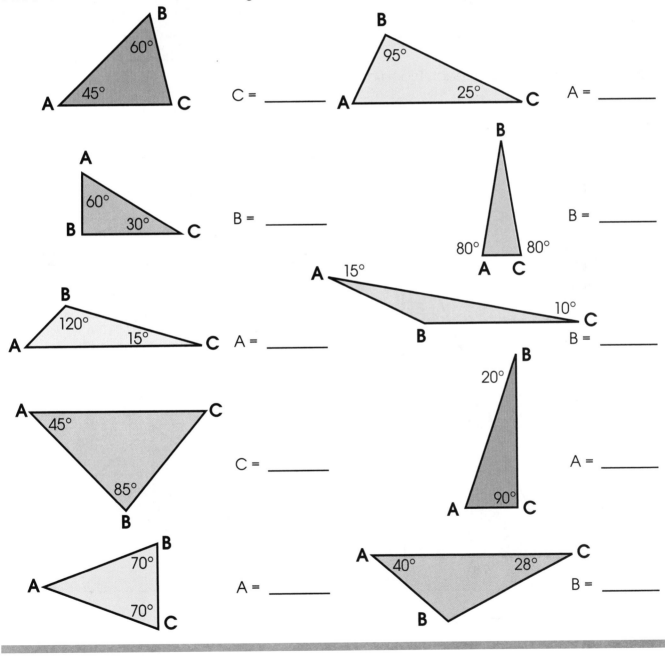

C = _____

A = _____

B = _____

B = _____

A = _____

B = _____

C = _____

A = _____

A = _____

B = _____

Name: _____

Area of a Triangle

The area of a triangle is found by multiplying $\frac{1}{2}$ times the base times the height.
$A = \frac{1}{2} \times b \times h$

Example:

$\overline{CD}$ is the height.   4 in.

$\overline{AB}$ is the base.   8 in.

Area = $\frac{1}{2} \times 4 \times 8 = \frac{32}{2} = 16$ sq. in.

Directions: Find the area of each triangle.

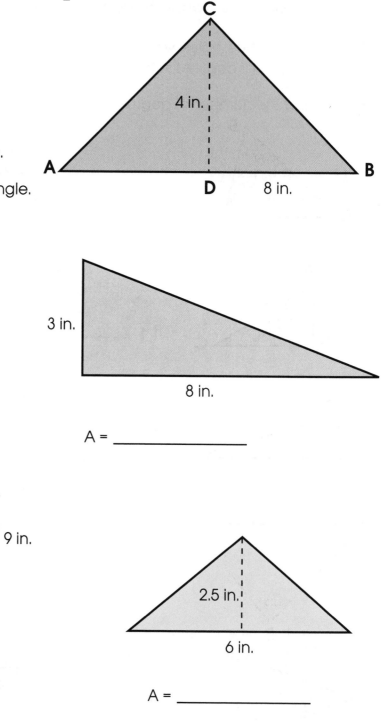

A = _____

A = _____

A = _____

A = _____

Estimating Area

Estimating area means giving an approximate number of square units in a figure.

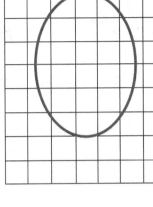

Example: The Andrews family is building a swimming pool. To find out how much material they will need, they must estimate the area of the pool.

Step 2: Count the number of partial squares: 12

Step 3: Divide the number of partial squares by 2: 6

Step 4: Add $1/2$ the number of the partial squares to the number of whole squares. Round to the nearest whole number.

14 + 6 = 20

Directions: Follow the steps to estimate the area of each figure. Round the answer to the nearest whole number.

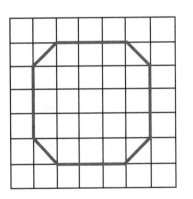

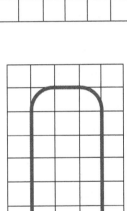

whole units 21

partial units 4

A = _____

whole units 17

partial units 4

A = _____

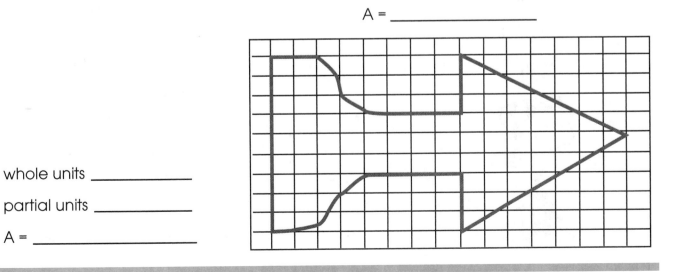

whole units _____

partial units _____

A = _____

Name: _____

Space Figures

Space figures are figures whose points are in more than one plane. Cubes and cylinders are space figures.

rectangular prism   **cone**   **cube**   **cylinder**   **sphere**   **pyramid**

A **prism** has two identical, parallel bases.

All of the faces on a **rectangular prism** are rectangles.

A **cube** is a prism with six identical, square faces.

A **pyramid** is a space figure whose base is a polygon and whose faces are triangles with a common vertex—the point where two rays meet.

A **cylinder** has a curved surface and two parallel bases that are identical circles.

A **cone** has one circular, flat face and one vertex.

A **sphere** has no flat surface. All points are an equal distance from the center.

Directions: Circle the name of the figure you see in each of these familiar objects

	cone	sphere	cylinder
	cone	sphere	cylinder
	cube	rectangular prism	pyramid
	cone	pyramid	cylinder

Name: _____

Review

Directions: Find the perimeter and area of each figure.

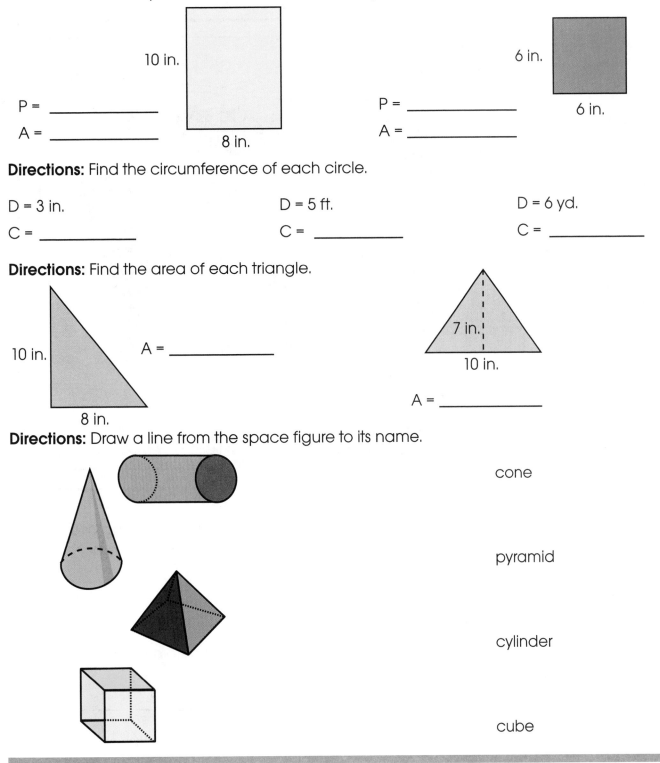

10 in.

P = _____

A = _____

8 in.

6 in.

P = _____

A = _____

6 in.

Directions: Find the circumference of each circle.

D = 3 in.

C = _____

D = 5 ft.

C = _____

D = 6 yd.

C = _____

Directions: Find the area of each triangle.

10 in.

A = _____

8 in.

7 in.

10 in.

A = _____

Directions: Draw a line from the space figure to its name.

cone

pyramid

cylinder

cube

Name: _____

Measurement

Directions: Use the map to help plan a day at the zoo.

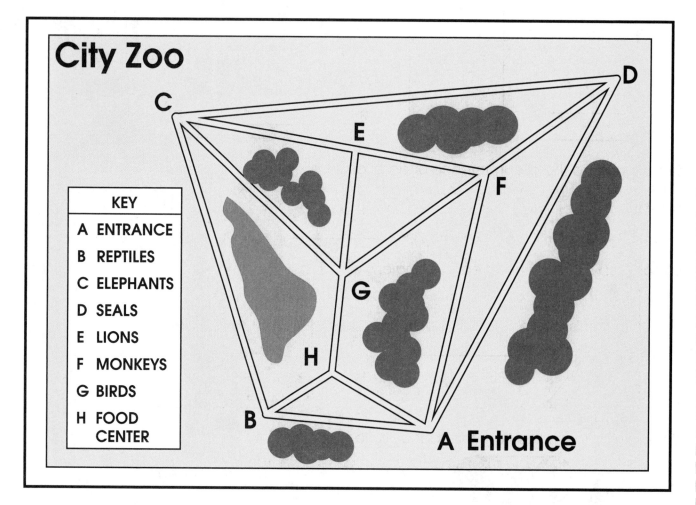

The class is going to the zoo. They want to see the elephants, monkeys, lions and birds before lunch at the food center. What is a logical path to travel from A to H to see the animals?

A ➔ _____   E ➔ _____   G ➔ H

What path would you take to see the seals, reptiles and monkeys before leaving the zoo?

_____

Name: _____

Measurement

Directions: Use the map on the previous page to answer these questions.

What is the shortest path to follow from the front gate in order to see the elephants, monkeys and birds?

_____

Traveling from the food center, which animal arena is farthest away? _____

Which is closest? _____

Which animals would you see if you only traveled the path on the perimeter of the zoo?

_____

What shape would you create if you followed the path from A to D to F and back to A?

_____

Is it possible to create a square by following any of the paths? If so, which ones?

_____

Name: _____

Length

Inches, **feet**, **yards** and **miles** are used to measure length in the United States.

12 inches = 1 foot (ft.)

3 feet = 1 yard (yd.)

36 inches = 1 yard

1,760 yards = 1 mile (mi.)

Directions: Circle the best unit to measure each object. The first one has been done for you.

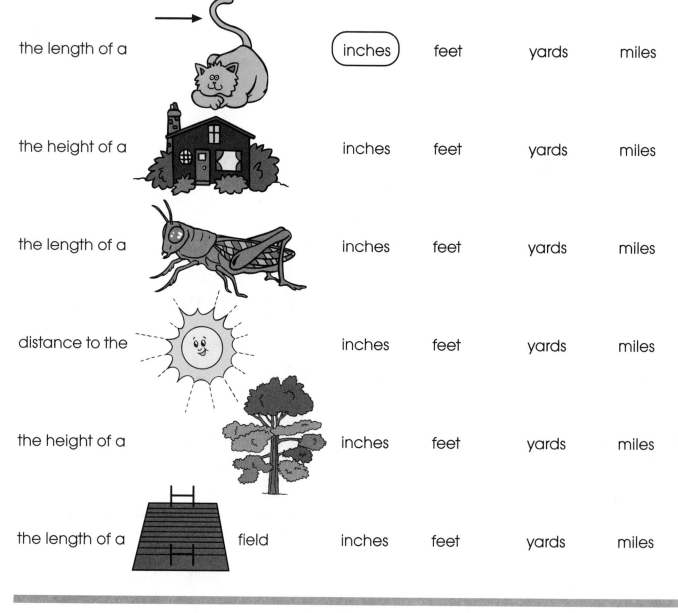

the length of a	(inches)	feet	yards	miles
the height of a	inches	feet	yards	miles
the length of a	inches	feet	yards	miles
distance to the	inches	feet	yards	miles
the height of a	inches	feet	yards	miles
the length of a field	inches	feet	yards	miles

Length

Units of measure can be converted (changed) from one unit to another.

Example: The distance from the teacher's desk to the door is 24 feet.

24 ft. = $\underline{8\ yd.}$

Directions: Convert the units of measure using the previous page.

The distance from the plants to the computer is 5 yd.

5 yd. = _____ ft.

The teacher's desk is 5 ft. long.

5 ft. = _____ in.

The Reading Corner is 3 yd. wide.

3 yd. = _____ in.

The distance from the computer to the door is 9 yd.

9 yd. = _____ ft.

Classroom Map

Plants

Computer

Teacher's Desk

Door

Reading Corner

Length

Directions: Use a ruler to find the shortest paths. Round your measurement to the nearest quarter inch. Then convert to yards using the scale.

Scale: 1 inch = 100 yards

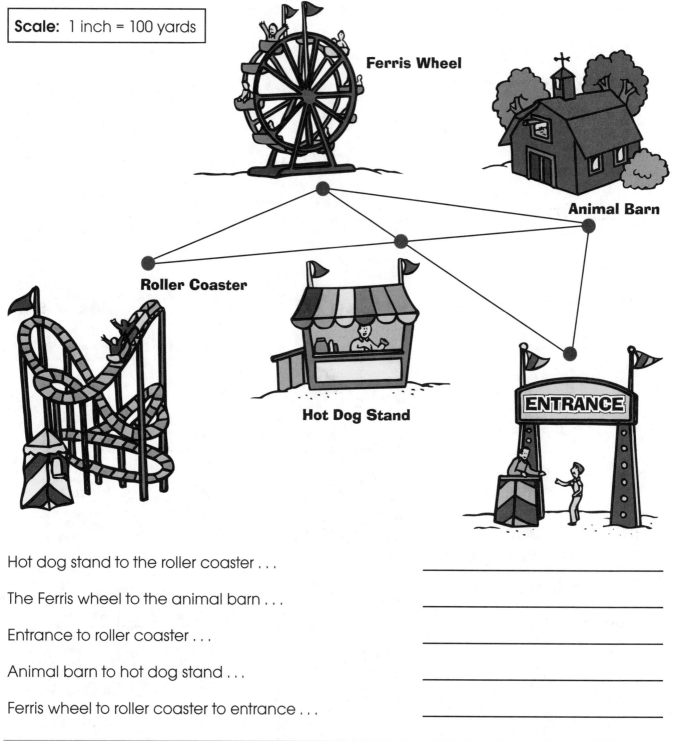

Hot dog stand to the roller coaster . . . _____

The Ferris wheel to the animal barn . . . _____

Entrance to roller coaster . . . _____

Animal barn to hot dog stand . . . _____

Ferris wheel to roller coaster to entrance . . . _____

82

Name: _____

Length: Metric

Millimeters, **centimeters**, **meters** and **kilometers** are used to measure length in the metric system.

> 1 meter = 39.37 inches
>
> 1 kilometer = about $\frac{5}{8}$ mile
>
> 10 millimeters = 1 centimeter (cm)
>
> 100 centimeters = 1 meter (m)
>
> 1,000 meters = 1 kilometer (km)

Directions: Circle the best unit to measure each object. The first one has been done for you.

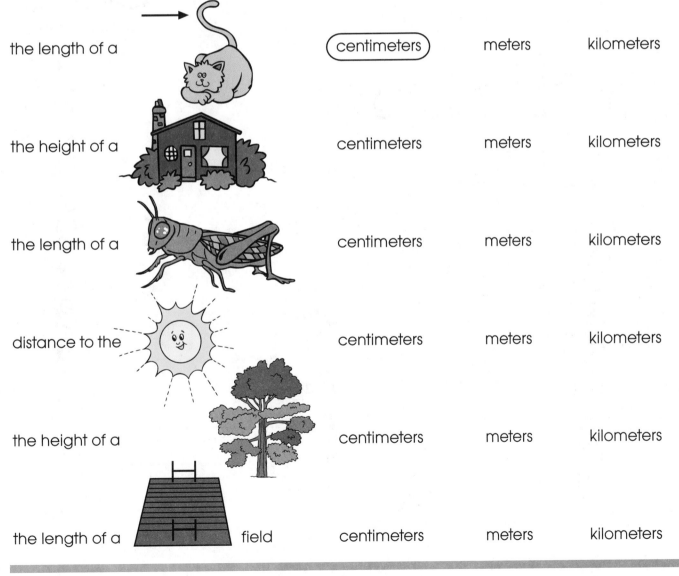

the length of a	(centimeters)	meters	kilometers
the height of a	centimeters	meters	kilometers
the length of a	centimeters	meters	kilometers
distance to the	centimeters	meters	kilometers
the height of a	centimeters	meters	kilometers
the length of a field	centimeters	meters	kilometers

Name: _____

Length: Metric

2.54 centimeters = 1 inch

1 millimeter = $\frac{1}{10}$ centimeter

Directions: Use a metric ruler to measure the length of each object.

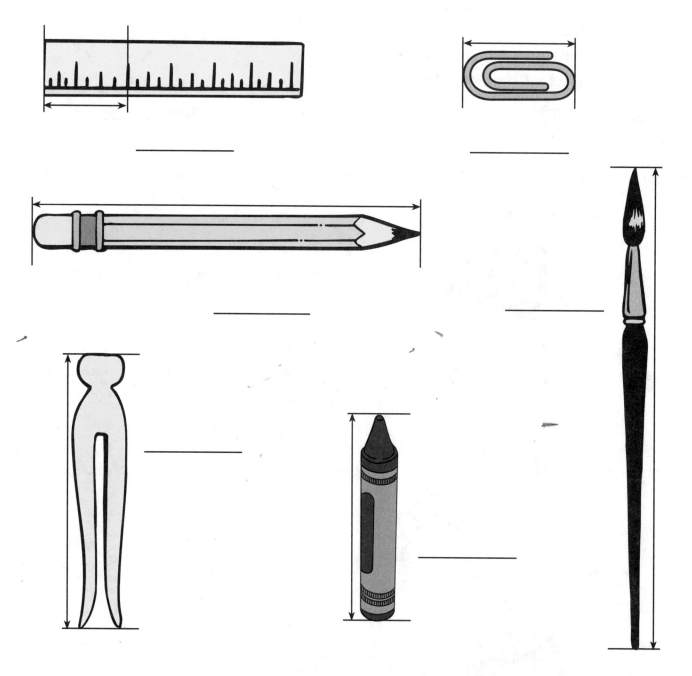

Name: _____

Weight

Ounces, pounds and **tons** are used to measure weight in the United States.

16 ounces = 1 pound (lb.)
2,000 pounds = 1 ton (tn.)

Directions: Circle the most reasonable estimate for the weight of each object. The first one has been done for you.

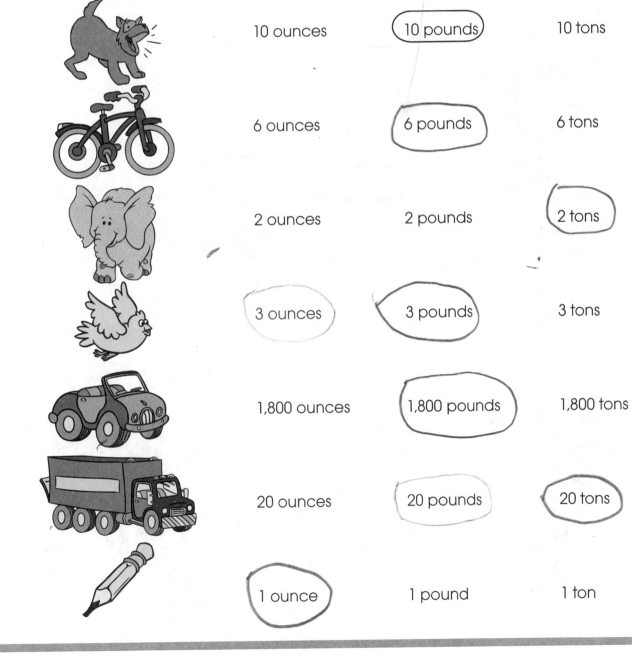

10 ounces	(10 pounds)	10 tons
6 ounces	(6 pounds)	6 tons
2 ounces	2 pounds	(2 tons)
(3 ounces)	(3 pounds)	3 tons
1,800 ounces	(1,800 pounds)	1,800 tons
20 ounces	(20 pounds)	(20 tons)
(1 ounce)	1 pound	1 ton

Name: _____

Weight: Metric

Grams and **kilograms** are units of weight in the metric system. A paper clip weighs about 1 gram. A kitten weighs about 1 kilogram.

1 kilogram (kg) = about 2.2 pounds

1,000 grams (g) = 1 kilogram

Directions: Circle the best unit to weigh each object.

Name: _____

Capacity

The **fluid ounce**, **cup**, **pint**, **quart** and **gallon** are used to measure capacity in the United States.

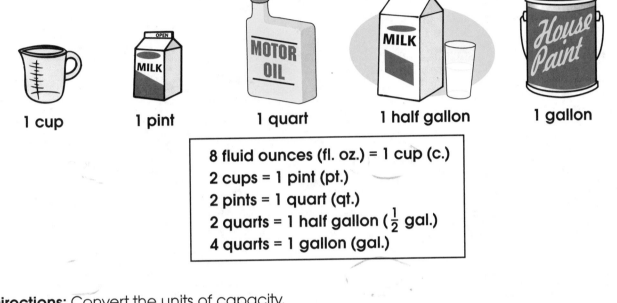

1 cup   1 pint   1 quart   1 half gallon   1 gallon

8 fluid ounces (fl. oz.) = 1 cup (c.)
2 cups = 1 pint (pt.)
2 pints = 1 quart (qt.)
2 quarts = 1 half gallon ($\frac{1}{2}$ gal.)
4 quarts = 1 gallon (gal.)

Directions: Convert the units of capacity.

13 gal. = _____ qt.   10 pt. = _____ c.   12 c. = _____ pt.

4 gal. = _____ qt.   16 qt. = _____ gal.   5 c. = _____ pt.

36 pt. = _____ gal.   12 qt. = _____ pt.   6 gal. = _____ pt.

16 c. = _____ qt.   32 oz. = _____ c.   16 oz. = _____ pt.

Name: _____

Capacity: Metric

Milliliters and liters are units of capacity in the metric system. A can of soda contains about 350 milliliters of liquid. A large plastic bottle contains 1 liter of liquid. A liter is about a quart.

1,000 milliliters (mL) = 1 liter (L)

Directions: Circle the best unit to measure each liquid.

milliliters
liters

milliliters
liters

milliliters
liters

milliliters
liters

milliliters
liters

milliliters
liters

milliliters
liters

milliliters
liters

milliliters
liters

milliliters
liters

Name: _____

Comparing Measurements

Directions: Use the symbols greater than (>), less than (<) or equal to (=) to complete each statement.

10 inches _____ 10 centimeters

40 feet _____ 120 yards

25 grams _____ 25 kilograms

16 quarts _____ 4 gallons

2 liters _____ 2 milliliters

16 yards _____ 6 meters

3 miles _____ 3 kilometers

20 centimeters _____ 20 meters

85 kilograms _____ 8 grams

2 liters _____ 1 gallon

Name: _____

Temperature: Fahrenheit

Degrees Fahrenheit (°F) is a unit for measuring temperature.

Directions: Write the temperature in degrees Fahrenheit (°F).

Example:

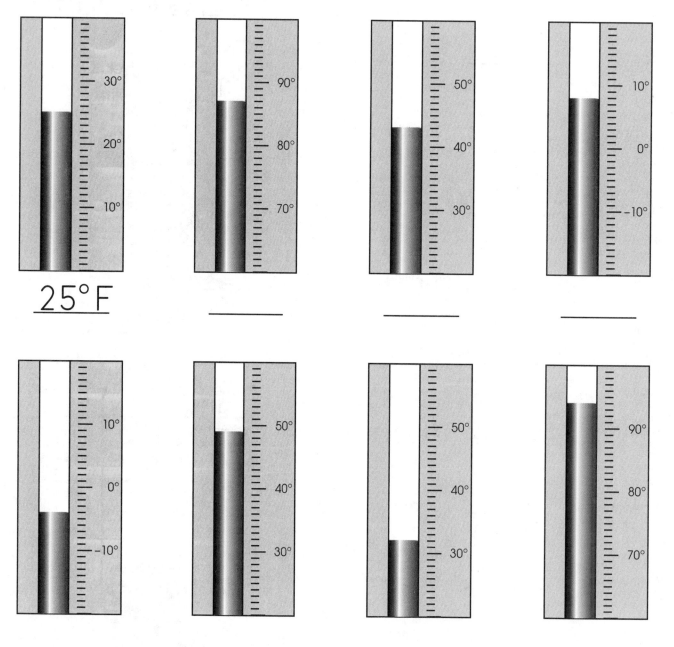

$\underline{25°F}$

_____   _____   _____

_____   _____   _____   _____

Temperature: Celsius

Degrees Celsius (°C) is a unit for measuring temperature in the metric system.

Directions: Write the temperature in degrees Celsius (°C).

Example:

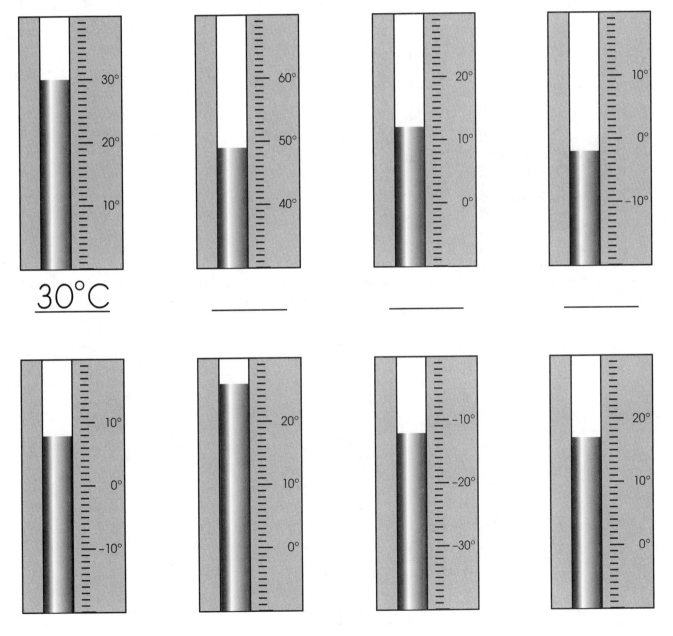

30°C _____   _____   _____   _____

_____   _____   _____   _____

Name: _____

Review

Directions: Name three common objects that are measured in metric units. Draw a picture of the object and tell what metric unit of measure is used.

Example: Bleach — 3 liters

Name: _____

Review

Directions: Write the best unit to measure each item: inch, foot, yard, mile, ounce, pound, ton, fluid ounce, cup, pint, quart or gallon.

distance from New York to Chicago   _____

weight of a goldfish   _____

height of a building   _____

water in a large fish tank   _____

glass of milk   _____

weight of a whale   _____

length of a pencil   _____

distance from first base to second base   _____

distance traveled by a space shuttle   _____

length of a soccer field   _____

amount of paint needed to cover a house   _____

material needed to make a dress   _____

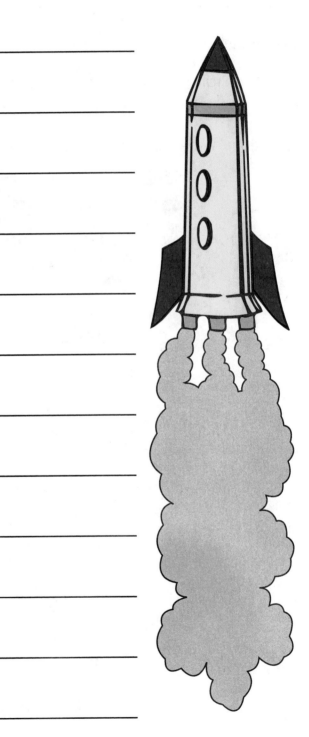

Name: _____

Ratio

A **ratio** is a comparison of two quantities.

Ratios can be written three ways: 2 to 3 or 2 : 3 or $\frac{2}{3}$. Each ratio is read: two to three.

Example:

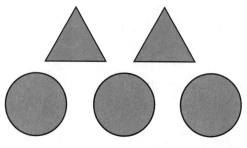

The ratio of triangles to circles is 2 to 3.

The ratio of circles to triangles is 3 to 2.

Directions: Write the ratio that compares these items.

ratio of tulips to cacti _____

ratio of cubes to triangles _____

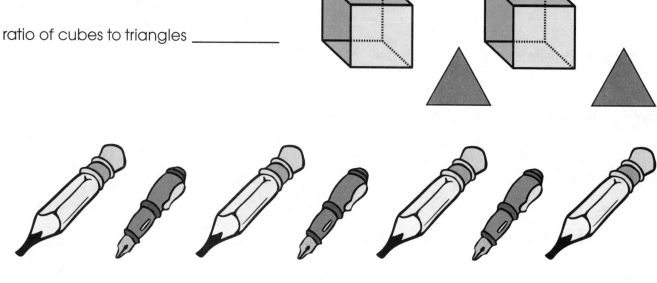

ratio of pens to pencils _____

Name: _____

Percent

Percent is a ratio meaning "per hundred." It is written with a % sign. 20% means 20 percent or 20 per hundred.

Example:

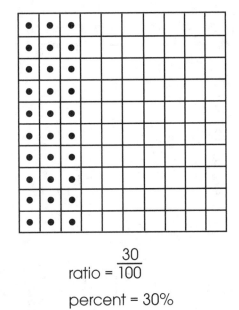

ratio = $\frac{30}{100}$

percent = 30%

ratio = _____

percent = _____

Directions: Write the percent for each ratio.

Book Sale

$\frac{7}{100}$ =	$\frac{38}{100}$ =
$\frac{63}{100}$ =	$\frac{3}{100}$ =
$\frac{40}{100}$ =	$\frac{1}{5}$ =

The school received 100 books for the Book Fair. It sold 43 books.

What is the percent of books sold to books received? _____

Name: _____

Ratio and Percent

A ratio is used to show the relationship between two things. A percent is a way of stating a ratio as compared to 100.

Animals at the Zoo

Type of Animal	Total Number of Animals	Number of Adults	Number of Young
Reptiles	15	8	7
Elephants	6	4	2
Seals	12	8	4
Lions	7	6	1
Monkeys	45	30	15
Tropical Birds	15	12	3

Directions: Use the chart to find the ratios.

Seals to elephants _____

Adult monkeys to young monkeys _____

Lions to tropical birds _____

Mammals to reptiles _____

Young reptiles to young mammals _____

Monkeys to seals _____

Total adults to total young _____

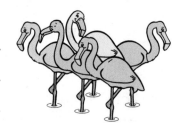

Directions: Use the chart to find the percents.

What percent of all the animals are mammals? _____

What percent of the zoo animals are adults? _____

What percent of the animals have feathers? _____

What percent of the animals reproduce by laying eggs? _____

What percent of the animals are cold-blooded? _____

Probability

Probability is the ratio of favorable outcomes to possible outcomes of an experiment.

Vehicle	Number Sold
4 door	26
2 door	18
Sport	7
Van	12
Wagon	7
Compact	5
Total	75

Example:

This table records vehicle sales for 1 month. What is the probability of a person buying a van?

number of vans sold = 12   total number of cars = 75

The probability that a person will choose a van is 12 in 75 or $\frac{12}{75}$.

Directions: Look at the chart of flowers sold in a month. What is the probability that a person will buy each?

Roses   _____

Tulips   _____

Violets _____

Orchids _____

Flowers	Number Sold
Roses	48
Tulips	10
Violets	11
Orchids	7
Total	76

How would probability help a flower store owner keep the correct quantity of each flower in the store?

_____

_____

_____

Calculators

A **calculator** is a machine that rapidly does addition, subtraction, multiplication, division and other mathematical functions.

Example:

Carlos got 7 hits in 20 "at bats."

$$\frac{7}{20} = \frac{35}{100} = 35\%$$

To use a calculator:

Step 1: Press 7.

Step 2: Press the ÷ symbol.

Step 3: Press 20.

Step 4: Press the = symbol.

Step 5: 0.35 appears.
0.35 = 35%.

Directions: Use a calculator to find the percent of hits to the number of "at bats" for each baseball player. Round your answer to two digits. If your calculator displays the answer 0.753, round it to 0.75 or 75%.

Player	Hits	At Bats	Percent
Carlos	7	20	35%
Troy	3	12	_____
Sasha	4	14	_____
Dan	8	18	_____
Jaye	5	16	_____
Keesha	9	17	_____
Martin	11	16	_____
Robi	6	21	_____
Devan	4	15	_____

Who is most likely to get a hit? _____

Name: _____

Finding Percents

Find percent by dividing the number you have by the number possible.

Example:

15 out of 20 possible:

$$20 \overline{)15.00} \quad \frac{0.75}{} = 75\%$$

$$\begin{array}{r} 0.75 \\ 20\overline{)15.00} \\ \underline{-140} \\ 100 \\ \underline{100} \end{array}$$

Annie has been keeping track of the scores she earned on each spelling test during the grading period.

Directions: Find out each percentage grade she earned. The first one has been done for you.

Week	Number Correct		Total Number of Words	Score in Percent
1	14	(out of)	20	70%
2	16		20	_____
3	18		20	_____
4	12		15	_____
5	16		16	_____
6	17		18	_____
Review Test	51		60	_____

If Susan scored 5% higher than Annie on the review test, how many words did she get right?   _____

Carrie scored 10% lower than Susan on the review test. How many words did she spell correctly?   _____

Of the 24 students in Annie's class, 25% had the same score as Annie. Only 10% had a higher score. What percent had a lower score?   _____

Is that answer possible? _____

Why? _____

Name: _____

Locating Points on a Grid

Coordinates help locate places on maps at the point where their imaginary lines intersect.

Directions: Write the coordinates for the location of each object. The first one has been done for you.

Doll ___3, T___   Cat _16, V_   Dog _14,B_

Bike _16,V_   Skateboard _8,L_   Bird _4,c_

Jump Rope _22,R_   Baseball Glove _18,K_   Rabbit _20,c_

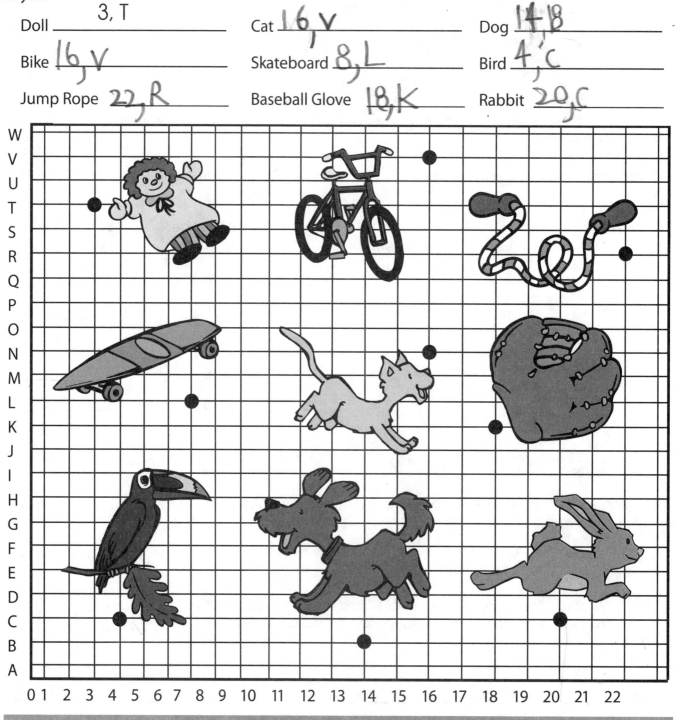

Name: _____

Locating Points on a Grid

To locate points on a grid, read the first coordinate and follow it to the second coordinate.

Example: 3, C

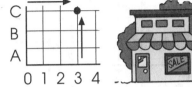

Directions: Maya is new in town. Help her learn the way around her new neighborhood. Place the following locations on the grid below.

Grocery	10, C
Home	2, B
School	12, A
Playground	13, B
Library	6, D
Bank	1, G
Post Office	7, E
Ice-Cream Shop	3, D

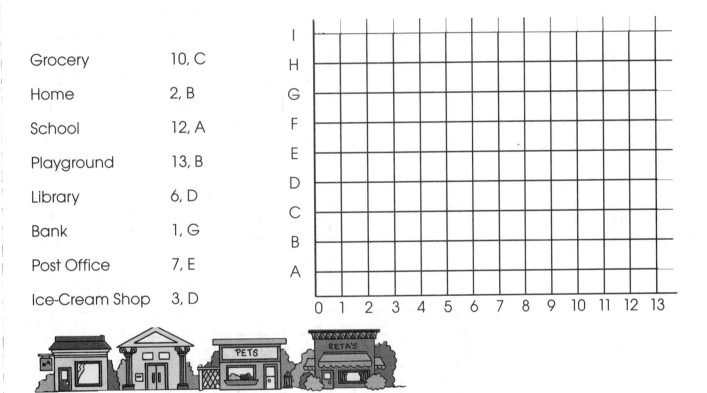

Is her home closer to the bank or the grocery? _____

Does she pass the playground on her way to school? _____

If she needs to stop at the library after school, will she
be closer to home or farther away? _____

Name: _____

Locating Points on a Grid

Directions: Draw the lines as directed from point to point for each graph.

Draw a line from:

- F,7 to D,1
- D,1 to I,6
- I,6 to N,8
- N,8 to M,3
- M,3 to F,1
- F,1 to G,4
- G,4 to E,4
- E,4 to B,1

- B,1 to A,8
- A,8 to D,11
- D,11 to F,9
- F,9 to F,7
- F,7 to I,9
- I,9 to I,6
- I,6 to F,7

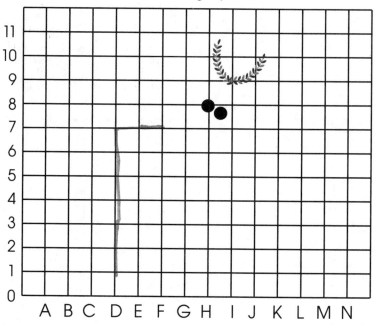

Draw a line from:

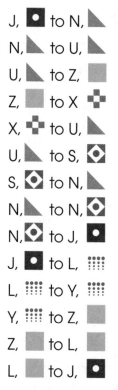

J, ⬛ to N, ◣
N, ◣ to U, ◣
U, ◣ to Z, ⬜
Z, ⬜ to X, ✚
X, ✚ to U, ◣
U, ◣ to S, ◉
S, ◉ to N, ◣
N, ◣ to N, ◉
N, ◉ to J, ⬛
J, ⬛ to L, ⸬
L, ⸬ to Y, ⸬
Y, ⸬ to Z, ⬜
Z, ⬜ to L, ⬜
L, ⬜ to J, ⬛

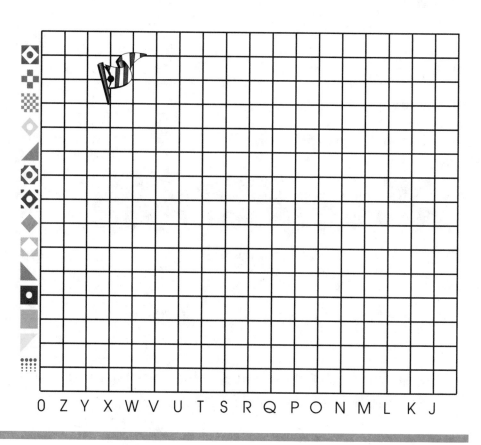

102

Name: _____

Graphs

A **graph** is a drawing that shows information about changes in numbers.

Directions: Use the graph to answer the questions.

Line Graph   **Temperatures for 1 Year**

```
100°  ------------------------------------●------------------
 90°  ----------------------------------/--●-----------------
 80°  ---------------------------------/-----●---------------
 70°  ----------------●------●--------/---------\------------
 60°  ---------------/--------\------/------------●----------
 50°  -------●------/----------\----/--------------\---------
 40°  ●----/--\----/------------\--/----------------●--------
 30°  ------------●------------------------------------●-----
 20°  ------------------------------------------------------
 10°  ------------------------------------------------------
  0°
      Jan. Feb. March April May June July Aug. Sept. Oct. Nov. Dec.
```

Which month was the coldest?   _____

Which month was the warmest?   _____

Which three months were 40 degrees?   _____

How much warmer was it in May than October?   _____

Bar Graph

Home Runs
→

```
50 |                    ____
40 |                   |    |
30 |                   |    |
20 |  ____             |    |
10 | |    |     ____   |    |
   |_|____|____|____|__|____|
     Red    Blue   Green
```

Teams →   Red   Blue   Green

How many home runs did the Green team hit? _____

How many more home runs did the Green team
hit than the Red team and Blue team combined? _____

Name: _____

Graphs

Directions: Read each graph and follow the directions.

List the names of the students from the shortest to the tallest.

1. _____   4. _____

2. _____   5. _____

3. _____   6. _____

Heights of Students

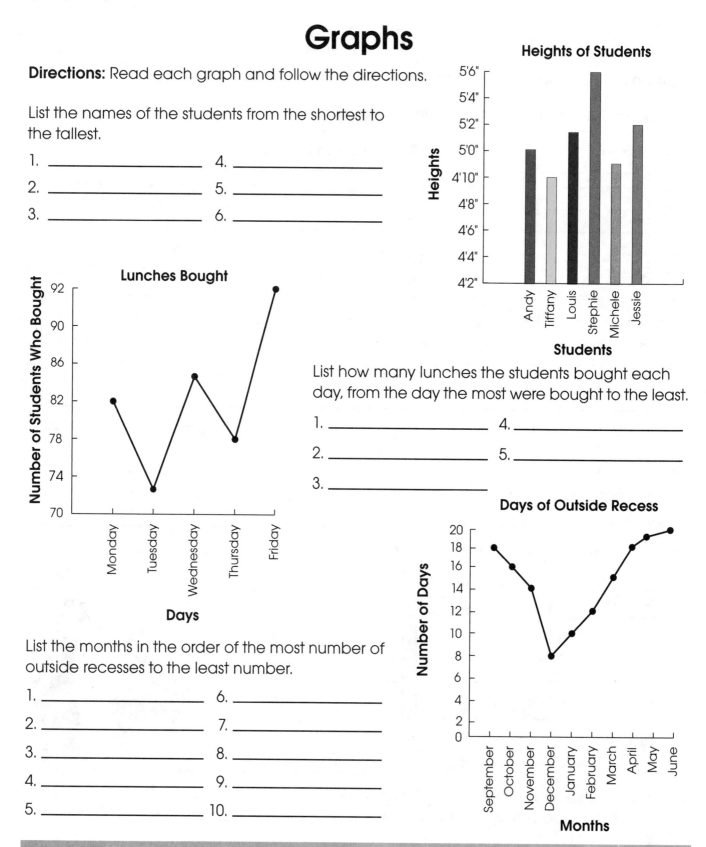

List how many lunches the students bought each day, from the day the most were bought to the least.

1. _____   4. _____

2. _____   5. _____

3. _____

List the months in the order of the most number of outside recesses to the least number.

1. _____   6. _____

2. _____   7. _____

3. _____   8. _____

4. _____   9. _____

5. _____   10. _____

104

Graphs

Directions: Complete the graph using the information in the table.

Student	Books read in February
Sue	20
Joe	8
Peter	12
Cindy	16
Dean	15
Carol	8

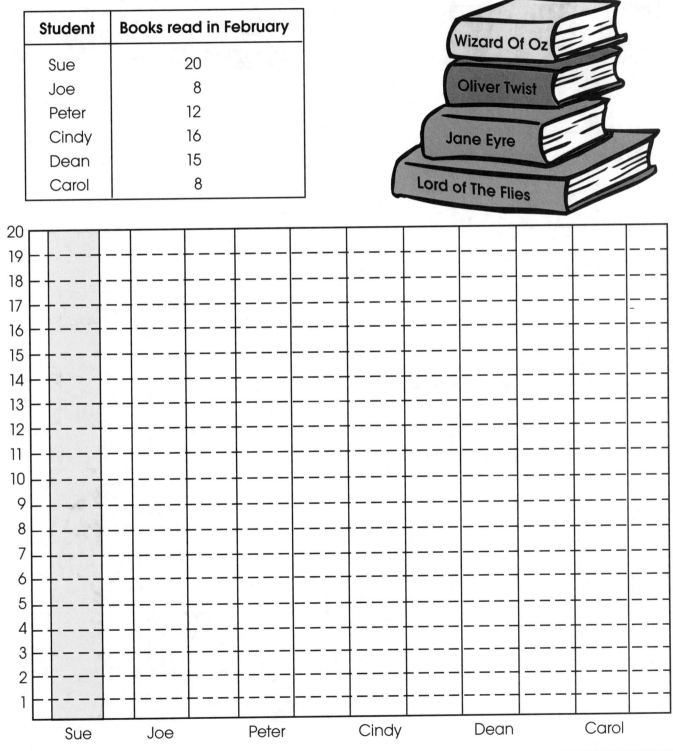

	Sue	Joe	Peter	Cindy	Dean	Carol
20						
19						
18						
17						
16						
15						
14						
13						
12						
11						
10						
9						
8						
7						
6						
5						
4						
3						
2						
1						

Name: _____

Review

Directions: Write a ratio for each.

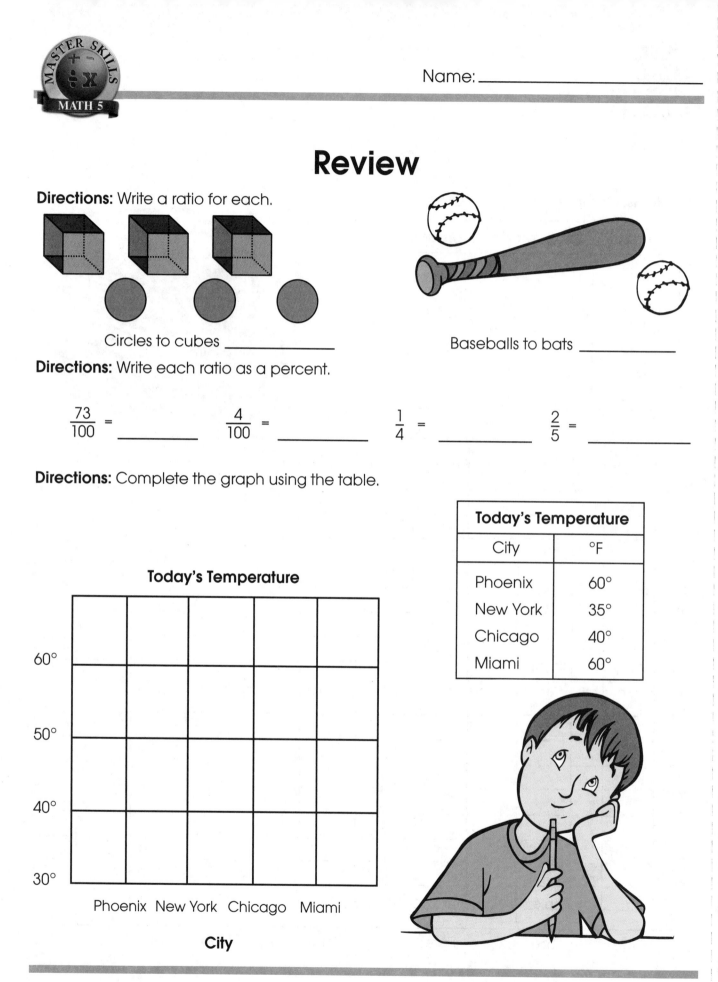

Circles to cubes _____

Baseballs to bats _____

Directions: Write each ratio as a percent.

$\frac{73}{100}$ = _____ $\frac{4}{100}$ = _____ $\frac{1}{4}$ = _____ $\frac{2}{5}$ = _____

Directions: Complete the graph using the table.

Today's Temperature	
City	°F
Phoenix	60°
New York	35°
Chicago	40°
Miami	60°

Today's Temperature

60°

50°

40°

30°

Phoenix   New York   Chicago   Miami

City

Glossary

Addition: "Putting together" two or more numbers to find the sum.

Angle: Two rays with the same end point.

Area: The number of square units in a figure.

Calculator: A machine that rapidly does addition, subtraction, multiplication, division and other mathematical functions.

Celsius: A measurement of temperature in the metric system.

Centimeter (cm): A metric measurement of length. There are 2.54 centimeters in an inch.

Circumference: The distance around a circle.

Cone: A space figure with one circular, flat face and one vertex.

Congruent: Figures with identical shapes but different orientations (facing in different directions).

Cube: A space figure with six square faces.

Cup (c.): A measurement of capacity equal to 8 fluid ounces.

Cylinder: A space figure with a curved surface and two parallel bases that are identical circles.

Decimal: A number with one or more places to the right of a decimal point, such as 6.5 or 2.25.

Denominator: The number below the fraction bar in a fraction.

Diameter: A line segment that passes through the center of a circle and has both end points on the circle.

Dividend: A number that is divided by another number in a division problem. In the problem 28 : 7 = 4, 28 is the dividend.

Division: The process of dividing a number into equal groups of smaller numbers.

Divisor: The number that is divided into the dividend in a division problem. In the problem 28 ÷ 7 = 4, 7 is the divisor.

Equation: A number sentence.

Estimate: To give an approximate rather than an exact answer.

Factors: The numbers multiplied together to give a product.

Fahrenheit: A measurement of temperature in degrees.

Foot (ft.): A measurement of length equal to 12 inches.

Fraction: A number that names part of a whole. Examples: $\frac{1}{2}$ and $\frac{1}{3}$

Gallon (gal.): A measurement of capacity equal to 4 quarts.

Geometry: The branch of mathematics that has to do with points, lines and shapes.

Greatest Common Factor (GCF): The largest number for a set of numbers that divides evenly into each number in the set.

Gram (g): A metric measurement of weight. 1,000 grams = 1 kilogram.

Graph: A drawing that shows information about changes in numbers.

Improper Fraction: A fraction in which the numerator is greater than its denominator.

Inch: A measurement of length. 12 inches = 1 foot.

Kilogram (kg): A metric measurement of weight equal to 1,000 grams.

Kilometer (km): A metric measure of distance equal to 1,000 meters.

Least Common Multiple (LCM): The smallest number other than 0 which is a multiple of each number.

Line: A collection of points on a straight path that goes on and on in opposite directions.

Liter (L): A metric measurement of capacity equal to about 1 quart.

Meter (m): A metric measurement of length equal to 39.37 inches.

Mile (mi.): A measurement of distance equal to 1,760 yards.

Milliliter (mL): A metric measurement of capacity. 1,000 milliliters = 1 liter.

Millimeter (mm): A metric measurement of length. 10 millimeters = 1 centimeter.

Mixed Number: A number written as a whole number and a fraction.

Multiple: The product of a specific number and any other number. Example: The multiples of 2 are 2 (2 x 1), 4 (2 x 2), 6, 8, 10, 12, and so on.

Multiplication: A process of quick addition of a number a certain number of times.

Numerator: The number above the fraction bar in a fraction.

Ounce (oz.): A measurement of weight. 16 ounces = 1 pound.

Percent: A ratio which means "per hundred."

Perimeter: The distance around an object found by adding the lengths of the sides.

Pi (π): Equal to approximately 3.14.

Pint (pt.): A measurement of capacity equal to 2 cups.

Place Value: Shown by where a digit is in a number.

Pound (lb.): A measurement of weight equal to 16 ounces.

Prime Number: A positive whole number which can only be divided evenly by itself or one.

Prism: A space figure with two identical, parallel bases.

Probability: The ratio of favorable outcomes to possible outcomes of an experiment.

Product: The answer of a multiplication problem.

Pyramid: A space figure whose base is a polygon and whose faces are triangles with a common vertex—the point where two rays meet.

Quart (qt.): A measurement of capacity equal to 4 cups or 2 pints.

Quotient: The answer of a division problem.

Radius: A line segment with one end point on the circle and the other end point at the center.

Ratio: A comparison of two quantities.

Ray: A part of a line with one end point that goes on and on in one direction.

Rectangle: A figure with four corners and four sides. Sides opposite each other are the same length.

Rectangular prism: A space figure. All of the faces are rectangles.

Remainder: The number left over in the quotient of a division problem.

Rounding: To express a number to the nearest ten, hundred, thousand and so on. Examples: round 18 up to 20; round 11 down to 10.

Segment: A part of a line having two end points.

Sphere: A space figure with no flat surface. All points are an equal distance from the center.

Square: A figure with four corners and four sides of the same length.

Subtraction: "Taking away" one number from another. Used to find the difference between two numbers.

Symmetrical: A shape that can be divided equally into two identical parts.

Ton (tn.): A measurement of weight equal to 2,000 pounds.

Triangle: A figure with three corners and three sides.

Volume: The number of cubic units inside a space figure.

Yard: A measurement of distance equal to 3 feet.

Answer Key

Place Value

The place value of a digit or numeral is shown by where it is in the number. In the number 1,234, 1 has the place value of thousands, 2 is hundreds, 3 is tens and 4 is ones.

Example: 1,250,000,000

Read: One billion, two hundred fifty million
Write: 1,250,000,000

Billions			Millions			Thousands			Ones		
h	t	o	h	t	o	h	t	o	h	t	o
		1,	2	5	0,	0	0	0,	0	0	0

Directions: Read the words. Then write the numbers.

twenty million, three hundred four thousand ___20,304,000___

five thousand, four hundred twenty-three ___5,423___

one hundred fifty billion, eight million,
one thousand, five hundred ___150,008,001,500___

sixty billion, seven hundred million,
one hundred thousand, three hundred twelve ___60,700,100,312___

four hundred million, fifteen thousand,
seven hundred one ___400,015,701___

six hundred ninety-nine million, four thousand,
nine hundred forty-two ___699,004,942___

Here's a game to play with a partner.

Write a ten-digit number using each digit, 0 to 9, only once. Do not show the number to your partner. Give clues like: "There is a five in the hundreds place." The clues can be given in any order. See if your partner can write the same number you have written.

3

Place Value

Directions: Draw a line to connect each number to its correct written form.

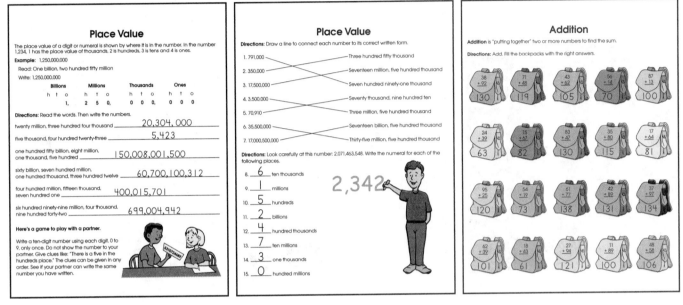

1. 791,000 — Three hundred fifty thousand
2. 350,000 — Seventeen million, five hundred thousand
3. 17,500,000 — Seven hundred ninety-one thousand
4. 3,500,000 — Seventy thousand, nine hundred ten
5. 70,910 — Three million, five hundred thousand
6. 35,500,000 — Seventeen billion, five hundred thousand
7. 17,000,500,000 — Thirty-five million, five hundred thousand

Directions: Look carefully at this number: 2,071,463,548. Write the numeral for each of the following places.

8. __6__ ten thousands
9. __1__ millions
10. __5__ hundreds
11. __2__ billions
12. __4__ hundred thousands
13. __7__ ten millions
14. __3__ one thousands
15. __0__ hundred millions

2,342

4

Addition

Addition is "putting together" two or more numbers to find the sum.

Directions: Add. Fill the backpacks with the right answers.

38 +92 = 130	71 +48 = 119	43 +62 = 105	56 +14 = 70	87 +13 = 100
24 +39 = 63	15 +67 = 82	83 +47 = 130	35 +80 = 115	17 +64 = 81
95 +25 = 120	54 +19 = 73	61 +77 = 138	42 +89 = 131	37 +97 = 134
62 +39 = 101	18 +43 = 61	27 +94 = 121	11 +89 = 100	48 +58 = 106

5

Addition

Teachers of an Earth Science class planned to take 50 students on an overnight hiking and camping experience. After planning the menu, they went to the grocery store for supplies.

Breakfast	Lunch	Dinner	Snacks
bacon	hot dogs/buns	pasta	crackers
eggs	apples	sauce	marshmallows
bread	chips	garlic bread	chocolate bars
cereal	juice	salad	cocoa mix
juice	granola bars	cookies	
$34.50	$ 52.15	$ 47.25	$ 23.40

Directions: Answer the questions. Write the total amount spent on food for the trip.

What information do you need to answer the question? ___the total for each meal and snacks added together___

What is the total? ___$157.30___

Directions: Add.

462 +574 = 1,036	918 +359 = 1,277	527 +582 = 1,109	386 +745 = 1,131	295 +764 = 1,059
397 +448 = 845	524 +725 = 1,249	906 +337 = 1,243	750 +643 = 1,393	891 +419 = 1,310
1,568 +2,341 = 3,909	3,214 +2,896 = 6,110	5,147 +4,285 = 9,432	7,259 +2,451 = 9,710	9,317 +3,583 = 12,900

6

Addition

Directions: Add.

1. Tourists travel to national parks to see the many animals which live there. Park Rangers estimate 384 buffalo, 282 grizzly bears and 426 deer are in the park. What is the total number of buffalo, bears and deer estimated in the park?
   ___1,092 buffalo, bears and deer___

2. Last August, 2,248 visitors drove motor homes into the campgrounds for overnight camping. 647 set up campsites with tents. How many campsites were there altogether in August?
   ___2,895 campsites___

3. During a 3-week camping trip, Tom and his family hiked 42 miles, took a 126 mile long canoeing trip and drove their car 853 miles. How many miles did they travel in all?
   ___1,021 miles___

4. Old Faithful is a geyser which spouts water high into the air. 10,000 gallons of water burst into the air regularly. Two other geysers spout 2,400 gallons of water during each eruption. What is the amount of water thrust into the air during one cycle?
   ___14,800 gallons___

5. Yellowstone National Park covers approximately 2,221,772 acres of land. Close by, the Grand Tetons cover approximately 310,350 acres. How many acres of land are there in these two parks?
   ___2,532,122 acres___

6. Hiking trails cover 486 miles, motor routes around the north rim total 376 miles, and another 322 miles of road allow visitors to follow a loop around the southern part of the park. How many miles of trails and roadways are there?
   ___1,184 miles___

7

Addition

Directions: Circle the lilypads with the correct answers to show the frogs the correct path to follow to join their mother on the other side of the pond.

52,913 +21,727 = 73,630	327 +418 = 735
14,525 +11,607 = 25,122	486 +583 = 964	74 +37 = 111
1,197 +423 = 1,620	375 +425 = 800	83,159 +12,432 = 95,581
73,482 +23,435 = 96,817	65,219 +25,098 = 90,317	870 +230 = 1,100
754 +347 = 1,091	26,492 +35,218 = 51,600	765 +245 = 1,010
49,639 +7,421 = 57,060	4,217 +12,982 = 17,199	8,951 +3,649 = 10,500

8

Addition

Bob the butcher is popular with the dogs in town. He was making a delivery this morning when he noticed he was being followed by two dogs. Bob tried to climb a ladder to escape from the dogs. Solve the following addition problems and shade in the answers on the ladder. If all the numbers are shaded when the problems have been solved, Bob made it up the ladder. Some answers may not be on the ladder.

1.
```
   986,145
   621,332
 + 200,008
 1,807,485
```
2.
```
 1,873,402
   925,666
     4,689
 2,803,757
```
3.
```
   506,328
   886,510
 + 342,225
 1,735,063
```

4.
```
    43,015
 2,811,604
 + 987,053
 3,841,672
```
5.
```
    18,443
   300,604
 + 999,999
 1,319,046
```
6.
```
     8,075
    14,608
 +  33,914
    56,597
```

7.
```
     9,162
     7,804
 + 755,122
   772,088
```
8.
```
    88,714
   213,653
 + 5,441,298
 5,743,665
```
9.
```
 3,244,662
 1,986,114
 + 521,387
 5,752,163
```

10.
```
     4,581
    22,983
 + 5,618,775
 5,646,339
```
11.
```
   818,623
       926
 + 3,260,004
 4,079,553
```
12.
```
    80,436
     9,159
 + 3,028,761
 3,118,356
```

Does Bob make it? __no__

Ladder:
```
1,319,046
2,803,757
5,743,665
3,118,356
56,597
4,079,553
1,807,485
2,943,230
18,344,666
1,735,063
5,752,163
896,316
3,841,672
5,646,339
```

9

Subtraction

Subtraction is "taking away" one number from another to find the difference between the two numbers.

Directions: Subtract.

```
  76      93      68      49      88      54
- 23    - 14    - 25    - 17    - 39    - 25
  53      79      43      32      49      29
```

Brent saved $75.00 of the money he earned delivering the local newspaper in his neighborhood. He wanted to buy a new bicycle that cost $139.00. How much more would he need to save in order to buy the bike?

__$64.00__

```
  38      74      67      92      43      85
- 29    - 25    - 49    - 35    - 26    - 37
   9      49      18      57      17      48
```

When Brent finally went to buy the bicycle, he saw a light and basket for the bike. He decided to buy them both. The light was $5.95 and the basket was $10.50. He gave the clerk a twenty dollar bill his grandmother had given him for his birthday. How much change did he get back?

__$3.55__

10

Subtraction

When working with larger numbers, it is important to keep the numbers lined up according to place value.

Subtract.

```
  398       543       491
- 149     - 287     - 311
  249       256       180
```

```
  786     1,825     4,172
- 597     - 495     - 2,785
  189     1,330     1,387
```

```
  8,391    63,852    24,107    52,900
- 5,492   - 34,765  - 19,350  - 43,081
  2,899    29,087    4,757     9,819
```

Eagle Peak is the highest mountain peak at Yellowstone National Park. It is 11,353 feet high. The next highest point at the park is Mount Washburn. It is 10,243 feet tall. How much higher is Eagle Peak?

__1,110 feet__

The highest mountain peak in North America is Mount McKinley, which stretches 20,320 feet toward the sky. Two other mountain ranges in North America have peaks at 10,302 feet and 8,194 feet. What is the greatest difference between the peaks?

__12,126 feet__

11

Checking Subtraction

You can check your subtraction by using addition.

Example:
```
  34,436    Check:    22,172
- 12,264            + 12,264
  22,172              34,436
```

Directions: Subtract. Then check your answers by adding.

```
  15,326   Check:     3,794
- 11,532            + 11,532
   3,794              15,326
```
```
  28,615   Check:     3,286
- 25,329            + 25,329
   3,286              28,615
```
```
  96,521   Check:    49,143
- 47,378            + 47,378
  49,143              96,521
```
```
  46,496   Check:    10,619
- 35,877            + 35,877
  10,619              46,496
```
```
  77,911   Check:    14,128
- 63,783            + 63,783
  14,128              77,911
```
```
 156,901   Check:    44,169
-112,732            +112,732
  44,169             156,901
```
```
 395,638   Check:   208,069
-187,569            +187,569
 208,069             395,638
```
```
  67,002   Check:    13,807
- 53,195            + 53,195
  13,807              67,002
```
```
  16,075   Check:       179
- 15,896            + 15,896
     179              16,075
```
```
  39,678   Check:    19,909
- 19,769            + 19,769
  19,909              39,678
```
```
  84,654   Check:    34,657
- 49,997            + 49,997
  34,657              84,654
```
```
  12,335   Check:     1,638
- 10,697            + 10,697
   1,638              12,335
```

During the summer, 158,941 people visited Yellowstone National Park. During the fall, there were 52,397 visitors. How many more visitors went to the park during the summer than the fall?

__106,544 visitors__

12

Addition and Subtraction

Directions: Check the answers. Write **T** if the answer is true and **F** if it is false. The first one has been done for you.

Example:
```
  48,973    Check:    35,856
- 35,856      F     + 13,118
  13,118              48,974
```

```
  18,264    Check:    36,157
+ 17,893      T     - 17,893
  36,157              18,264
```
```
 458,342    Check:   160,680
-297,652      F     +297,652
 160,680             458,332
```
```
  39,854    Check:    92,577
+ 52,713      F     - 52,713
  92,577              39,864
```
```
 631,928    Check:   174,313
-457,615      T     +457,615
 174,313             631,928
```
```
  14,389    Check:   107,976
+ 93,587      T     - 93,587
 107,976              14,389
```
```
 554,974    Check:   178,389
-376,585      T     +376,585
 178,389             554,974
```
```
  87,321    Check:    24,973
- 62,348      T     + 62,348
  24,973              87,321
```
```
 109,568    Check:   206,941
+ 97,373      T     - 97,373
 206,941             109,568
```

Directions: Read the story problem. Write the equation and check the answer.

A camper hikes 53,741 feet out into the wilderness. On his return trip he takes a shortcut, walking 36,752 feet back to his cabin. The <u>shortcut saves him 16,998 feet</u> of hiking. True or False?

```
  53,741     16,998
- 36,752    + 36,752
  16,989      53,750
```

13

Addition and Subtraction

Directions: Add or subtract to find the answers.

Eastland School hosted a field day. Students could sign up for a variety of events. 175 students signed up for individual races. Twenty two-person teams competed in the mile relay and 36 kids took part in the high jump. How many students participated in the activities?
__251 students__

Westmore School brought 42 students and 7 adults to the field day event. Northern School brought 84 students and 15 adults. There was a total of 300 students and 45 adults at the event. How many were from other schools?
__174 students 23 adults__

The Booster Club sponsored a concession stand during the day. Last year, they made $1,000 at the same event. This year they hoped to earn at least $1,250. They actually raised $1,842. How much more did they make than they had anticipated?
__$592.00__

Each school was awarded a trophy for participating in the field day's activities. The Booster Club planned to purchase three plaques as awards, but they only wanted to spend $150. The first place trophy they selected was $68. The second place award was $59. How much would they be able to spend on the third place award if they stay within their budgeted amount?
__$23.00__

The Booster Club decided to spend $1,000 to purchase several items for the school with the money they had earned. Study the list of items suggested and decide which combination of items they could purchase.

A. Swing set $425   __A+B+D__
B. Sliding board $263   __B+C+D__
C. Scoreboard $515   __A+C__
D. Team uniforms $180

14

Addition

When adding many numbers together, be sure to keep them lined up according to their place value.

Directions: Add. Use a calculator to check your answers.

408,107	75,310	708,302	6,700,241
31,641	89,632	40,927	9,334,300
9,111	1,542	20,085	3,017
400	736	343	4,322,119
+ 295	+ 922	+ 589	+ 7,384
449,554	**168,142**	**770,246**	**20,367,061**

215,106	3,892,442	5,312,612	8,700,370
69,015	318,712	680,325	804,304
5,446	76,698	46,659	17,009
621	7,361	7,360	7,919
+ 306	+ 567	+ 812	+ 250
290,494	**4,295,780**	**6,047,768**	**9,529,852**

954,432	6,935	12,897
126,243	12,897	64,382
27,591	69,473	29,318
8,920	43,190	13,269
+ 27	+ 48,579	+ 4,769
1,117,213	**181,074**	**124,635**

64,513
1,943
43,009
36,820
+ 32,692
178,977

15

Rounding

Rounding a number means to express it to the nearest ten, hundred, thousand and so on. When rounding a number to the nearest ten, if the number has five or more ones, round up. Round down if the number has four or fewer ones.

Examples:

Round to the nearest ten:	84 → 80	86 → 90
Round to the nearest hundred:	187 → 200	120 → 100
Round to the nearest thousand:	981 → 1,000	5,480 → 5,000

Directions: Round these numbers to the nearest ten.

87 → 90   53 → 50   48 → 50   32 → 30   76 → 80

Directions: Round these numbers to the nearest hundred.

168 → 200   243 → 200   591 → 600   743 → 700   493 → 500

Directions: Round these numbers to the nearest thousand.

895 → 1,000   3,492 → 3,000   7,521 → 8,000   14,904 → 15,000   62,387 → 62,000

City Populations	
City	Population
Cleveland	492,801
Seattle	520,947
Omaha	345,033
Kansas City	443,878
Atlanta	396,052
Austin	514,013

Directions: Use the city population chart to answer the questions.

Which cities have a population of about 500,000?
Cleveland, Seattle, Austin

Which city has a population of about 350,000?
Omaha

How many cities have a population of about 400,000? two

Which ones? Kansas City and Atlanta

16

Estimating

To **estimate** means to give an approximate rather than an exact answer. Rounding each number first makes it easy to estimate an answer.

Example:

93	90	321	300	1,859	2,000
+ 48	+ 50	+ 597	+ 600	− 997	− 1,000
	140		900		1,000

Directions: Estimate the sums and differences by rounding the numbers first.

68	70	12	10	89	90
+ 34	+ 30	+ 98	− 100	+ 23	+ 20
	100		110		110

638	600	281	300	271	300
− 395	− 400	− 69	− 100	− 126	− 100
	200		200		200

1,532	2,000	8,312	8,000	6,341	6,000
− 998	− 1,000	− 4,789	− 5,000	+ 9,286	+ 9,000
	1,000		3,000		15,000

Bonnie has $50 to purchase tennis shoes, a tennis racquet and tennis balls. Does she have enough money?

_____ yes

$23.00 $16.00 $3.00

17

Rounding and Estimating

Rounding numbers and estimating answers is an easy way of finding the approximate answer without writing out the problem or using a calculator.

Directions: Circle the correct answer.

Round to the nearest **ten**:

73 → (70) / 80   48 → 40 / (50)   65 → 60 / (70)

85 → (80) / 90   92 → (90) / 100   37 → 30 / (40)

Round to the nearest **hundred**:

139 → (100) / 200   782 → 700 / (800)   390 → (300) / 400

640 → (600) / 700   525 → (500) / 600   457 → 400 / (500)

Round to the nearest **thousand**:

1,375 → (1,000) / 2,000   21,800 → (21,000) / 22,000   36,240 → (36,000) / 37,000

Sam wanted to buy a new computer. He knew he only had about $1,200 to spend. Which of the following ones could he afford to buy?

$1,165 $1,279 $1,249

If Sam spent $39 on software for his new computer, $265 for a printer and $38 for a cordless mouse, about how much money did he need?
$40 + $300 + $40 = $380.00

18

Review

Directions: Add.

1. 45 + 50 = 95
2. 63 + 37 = 100
3. 25 + 60 = 85
4. 55 + 55 = 110
5. 72 + 28 = 100
6. 56 + 16 = 72
7. 90 + 43 = 133
8. 63 + 73 = 136
9. 92 + 18 = 110
10. 34 + 70 = 104
11. 75 + 75 = 150
12. 90 + 69 = 159

Anne ordered these items for breakfast at her favorite restaurant:

scrambled eggs
toast
orange juice
bacon strips

Specials
Eggs $2.50
Bacon $2.15
Toast $1.20
Juice $1.25

How much did she spend? $7.10

Anne paid for her breakfast with a ten-dollar bill. How much change should she get back? $2.90

Directions: Subtract.

13. 95 − 30 = 65
14. 125 − 50 = 75
15. 67 − 20 = 47
16. 140 − 80 = 60
17. 49 − 10 = 39
18. 78 − 30 = 48
19. 150 − 65 = 85
20. 185 − 90 = 95
21. 88 − 20 = 68
22. 92 − 16 = 76
23. 180 − 90 = 90
24. 250 − 75 = 175

19

Review

Directions: Add.

256	8,968	28,493	168,573
+ 538	+ 3,481	+ 38,975	+ 257,899
794	**12,449**	**67,468**	**426,472**

Directions: Subtract.

189,453	1,350,681	856,721	29,051
− 98,794	− 467,792	− 650,853	− 15,160
90,659	**882,889**	**205,868**	**13,891**

Directions: Draw a line to the number that has:

five ten millions — 1,950,783
six hundreds — 45,640
nine hundred thousands — 17,001
zero tens — 1,453,682,073

Directions: Round to the nearest

ten	83 → 80	48 → 50	77 → 80
hundred	4,848 → 4,800	5,443 → 5,400	8,501 → 8,500
thousand	2,920 → 3,000	18,458 → 18,000	179,642 → 180,000
million	1,891,403 → 2,000,000	3,499,999 → 3,000,000	

Directions: Estimate the sums and differences by rounding.

582	600	7,951	8,000	6,891	7,000	17,988	18,000
+ 175	+ 200	− 1,241	− 1,000	+ 578	+ 1,000	− 5,749	− 6,000
	800		7,000		8,000		12,000

20

Prime Numbers

Example: 3 is a prime number 3 ÷ 1 = 3 and 3 ÷ 3 = 1
Any other divisor will result in a mixed number or fraction.

An easy way to test a number to see if it is prime is to divide by 2 and 3. If the number can be divided by 2 or 3 without a remainder, it is not a prime number. (Exceptions, 2 and 3.)

Example:

11 cannot be divided evenly by 2 or 3. It can only be divided by 1 and 11. It is a prime number.

A prime number is a positive whole number which can be divided evenly only by itself or one.

Directions: Write the first 15 prime numbers. Test by dividing by 2 and by 3.

Prime Numbers:

2	3	5	7	11
13	17	19	23	29
31	37	41	43	47

How many prime numbers are there between 0 and 100? 25

21

Prime Numbers

Directions: Circle the prime numbers.

(71)	(3)	82	20	(43)	69
128	(97)	(23)	111	75	51
(13)	44	(137)	68	171	(83)
(61)	21	77	(101)	34	16
(2)	39	92	(17)	52	(29)
(19)	156	63	99	27	147
121	25	88	12	87	55
57	(7)	(139)	91	9	(37)
(67)	183	(5)	(59)	(11)	95

22

Multiples

A **multiple** is the product of a specific number and any other number. When you multiply two numbers, the answer is called the **product**.

Example:

The multiples of 2 are 2 (2 x 1), 4 (2 x 2), 6, 8, 10, 12, and so on.

The **least common multiple** (LCM) of two or more numbers is the smallest number other than 0 that is a multiple of each number.

Example:

Multiples of 3 are 3, 6, 9, 12, 15, 18, 21, 24, etc.
Multiples of 6 are 6, 12, 18, 24, 30, 36, 42, etc.
The multiples that 3 and 6 have in common are 6, 12, 18, 24.
The LCM of 3 and 6 is 6.

LCM

Directions: Write the first nine multiples of 3, 4, and 6. Write the LCM.

3: 3 6 9 12 15 18 21 24 27
4: 4 8 12 16 20 24 28 32 36
6: 6 12 18 24 30 36 42 48 54
LCM = 12

Directions: Write the first nine multiples of 2 and 5. Write the LCM.

2: 2 4 6 8 10 12 14 16 18
5: 5 10 15 20 25 30 35 40 45
LCM = 10

Directions: Find the LCM for each pair of numbers.

7 and 3 21   4 and 6 12   6 and 9 18
5 and 15 15   5 and 4 20   3 and 18 18

Directions: Fill in the missing numbers.

30 has multiples of 5 and 6 , of 2 and 15 , of 3 and 10 .

23

Factors

Factors are the numbers multiplied together to give a product. The **greatest common factor** (GCF) is the largest number for a set of numbers that divides evenly into each number in the set.

Example:

The factors of 12 are 3 x 4, 2 x 6 and 1 x 12.
We can write the factors like this: 3, 4, 2, 6, 12, 1.
The factors of 8 are 2, 4, 8, 1.
The common factors of 12 and 8 are 2 and 4 and 1.
The GCF of 12 and 8 is 4.

3 x 4   2 x 6   1 x 12

Directions: Write the factors of each pair of numbers. Then write the common factors and the GCF.

12: 1 2 3 4 6 12
15: 1 3 5 15
The common factors of 12 and 15 are 1 , 3 .
The GCF is 3

20: 1 2 4 5 10 20
10: 1 2 5 10
The common factors of 10 and 20 are 1 , 2 , 5 , 10 .
The GCF is 10

32: 1 2 4 8 16 32
24: 1 2 3 4 6 8 12 24
The common factors of 24 and 32 are 1 , 2 , 4 , 8 .
The GCF is 8

Directions: Write the GCF for the following pairs of numbers.

28 and 20 4   42 and 12 6
36 and 12 12   20 and 5 5

24

Factor Trees

A **factor tree** shows the prime factors of a number. A prime number, such as 7, has for its factors only itself and 1.

Example:

30
6 x 5   30 = 3 x 2 x 5
3 2 5   3, 2, and 5 are prime numbers.

Directions: Fill in the numbers in the factor trees.

25

Factor Trees

Directions: Fill in the numbers in the factor trees. The first one has been done for you.

13,720
140 x 98
10 x 14 x 7
5 x 2 x 7 x 1

192
8 x 24
2 x 4 x 6
1 x 2 x 2 x 3

1,125
75 x 15
15 x 5 x 3
3 x 5 x 1 x 3

26

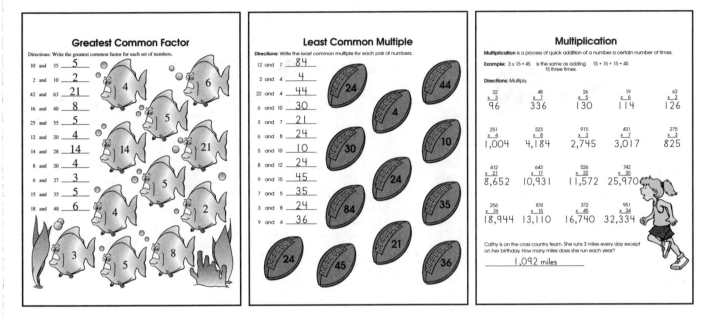

Greatest Common Factor

Directions: Write the greatest common factor for each set of numbers.

10 and 35 — 5
2 and 10 — 2
42 and 63 — 21
16 and 40 — 8
25 and 55 — 5
12 and 20 — 4
14 and 28 — 14
8 and 20 — 4
6 and 27 — 3
15 and 35 — 5
18 and 48 — 6

Fish: 4, 6, 5, 14, 21, 5, 2, 3, 5, 8

27

Least Common Multiple

Directions: Write the least common multiple for each pair of numbers.

12 and 7 — 84
2 and 4 — 4
22 and 4 — 44
6 and 10 — 30
3 and 7 — 21
6 and 8 — 24
5 and 10 — 10
8 and 12 — 24
9 and 15 — 45
7 and 5 — 35
3 and 8 — 24
9 and 4 — 36

Footballs: 24, 44, 4, 30, 10, 24, 84, 35, 21, 24, 45, 36

28

Multiplication

Multiplication is a process of quick addition of a number a certain number of times.

Example: 3 x 15 = 45   is the same as adding   15 + 15 + 15 = 45
15 three times.

Directions: Multiply.

32 x 3	48 x 7	26 x 5	19 x 6	63 x 2
96	336	130	114	126

251 x 4	523 x 8	915 x 3	431 x 7	275 x 3
1,004	4,184	2,745	3,017	825

412 x 21	643 x 17	526 x 22	742 x 35
8,652	10,931	11,572	25,970

256 x 74	874 x 15	372 x 45	951 x 34
18,944	13,110	16,740	32,334

Cathy is on the cross country team. She runs 3 miles every day except on her birthday. How many miles does she run each year?

1,092 miles

29

Multiplication

Directions: Multiply.

Josh decided to join a book club. He received a new book every 2 weeks. He read 40 pages every night during the first 2 weeks in order to finish one book. How many pages did he read?

560 pages

During the summer, he received 10 books in all. He read a total of 2,600 pages that summer. He read 65 pages each day that he read. How many days did it take him to read all 10 books?

40 days

The book company offered him a special deal. He could purchase five books for $49.00. He decided to buy 25 books at this special price. How much money did he need to send with his order?

$245.00

At the end of the year, Josh decided to share his books with a friend. His friend offered to pay him $3.00 for each book, but he only had $85.00 to spend. How many books could he buy?

28 books

Josh decided to join the book club for a second year. He challenged himself to read twice as many pages during the second summer. How many pages would he need to read?

5,200 pages

247 x 15	483 x 72	826 x 43	359 x 58	735 x 21
3,705	34,776	35,518	20,822	15,435

30

Multiplication

Be certain to keep the proper place value when multiplying by tens and hundreds.

Examples:

```
  143        250
x 262      x 150
  286        000
  858       1250
 286        250
37,466     37,500
```

Directions: Multiply.

701 x 308	621 x 538	348 x 200	597 x 424
215,908	334,098	69,600	253,128

537 x 189	416 x 727	682 x 472	180 x 340
101,493	302,432	321,904	61,200

878 x 638	267 x 196	893 x 214	907 x 428
560,164	52,332	191,102	388,196

An airplane flies 720 trips a year between the cities of Chicago and Columbus. Each trip is 375 miles. How many miles does the airplane fly each year?

270,000

31

Division

Division is the reverse of multiplication. It is the process of dividing a number into equal groups of smaller numbers.

Directions: Divide.

Greg had 936 marbles to share with his two brothers. If the boys divided them evenly, how many will each one get? 312 marbles

The marbles Greg kept were four different colors: blue, green, red and orange. He had the same number of each color. He divided them into two groups. One group had only orange marbles. The rest of the marbles were in the other group. How many marbles did he have in each group? orange 78 others 234

The **dividend** is the number to be divided by another number. In the problem 28 ÷ 7 = 4, 28 is the dividend.

The **divisor** is the number by which another number is divided. In the problem 28 ÷ 7 = 4, 7 is the divisor.

The **quotient** is the answer in a division problem. In the problem 28 ÷ 7 = 4, 4 is the quotient.

The **remainder** is the number left over in the quotient of a division problem. In the problem 29 ÷ 7 = 4 r1, 1 is the remainder.

Directions: Write the answers.

In the problem 25 ÷ 8 = 3 r1 . . .

What is the divisor? 8   What is the remainder? 1
What is the quotient? 3 r1   What is the dividend? 25

Directions: Divide.

9)2,025	6)2,508	3)225	5)400	2)1,156
225	418	75	80	578

32

Division

When dividing with remainders, the remainder must always be less than the divisor.

Example:
```
        244 r 23
26 ) 6,367
     52
     116
     104
     127
     104
      23
```

Directions: Divide.

```
        23 r 1           41 r 11          75 r 45          139 r 4
53 ) 1,220      37 ) 1,528      83 ) 6,270      26 ) 3,618


        27 r 1           91 r 6           133 r 30         94 r 48
14 ) 389        29 ) 2,645      60 ) 8,010      57 ) 5,406


        72 r 26          11 r 19          55 r 43          9 r 14
35 ) 2,546      43 ) 492        83 ) 4,608      19 ) 185
```

The Oregon Trail is 2,197 miles long. How long would it take a covered wagon traveling 20 miles a day to complete the trip?

__110 days__

33

Checking Division

Answers in division problems can be checked by multiplying.

Example:
```
         481 r 17    Check:      481
33 ) 15,890                    x  33
     132                        1443
     269                        1443
     264                       15,873
      50                     +    17
      33                       15,890
      17
```
Add the remainder

Directions: Divide and check your answers.

```
61 ) 2,736    Check:        44        73 ) 86,143   Check:      1,180
                          x 61                                 x  73
  44 r 52                 2,684       1,180 r 3               86,140
                         +  52                                +    3
                          2,736                               86,143


59 ) 9,390    Check:       159        43 ) 77,141   Check:      1793
                          x 59                                 x  43
  159 r 9                 9,381       1,793 r 42              77,099
                         +   9                                +   42
                          9,390                               77,141


33 ) 82,050   Check:     2,486        93 ) 84,039   Check:       903
                          x 33                                 x  93
 2,486 r 12              82,038        903 r 60              83,979
                        +   12                                +   60
                         82,050                               84,039
```

Denny has a baseball card collection. He has 13,789 cards. He wants to put the cards in a scrapbook that holds 15 cards on a page. How many pages does Denny need in his scrapbook? __920__

34

Equations

An **equation** is a number sentence. To solve an equation, always work from left to right unless numbers are in parentheses.

Directions: Write the answers to these equations. The first one has been done for you.

3 X 2 + 4 + 9 = __19__

4 X 2 X 8 ÷ 4 X 2 = __32__

9 ÷ 3 X 5 X 5 X 2 = __150__

7 X 4 X 3 ÷ 12 X 8 = __56__

20 X 3 ÷ 6 X 4 ÷ 5 = __8__

32 ÷ 8 X 4 X 4 ÷ 2 = __32__

14 ÷ 7 X 21 X 3 ÷ 3 = __42__

52 X 5 X 2 ÷ 5 X 7 = __728__

35

Multiplication and Division

Directions: Multiply or divide to find the answers.

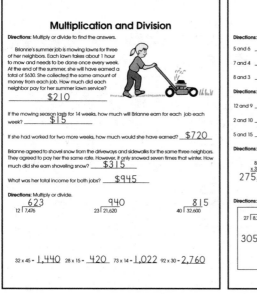

Brianne's summer job is mowing lawns for three of her neighbors. Each lawn takes about 1 hour to mow and needs to be done once every week. At the end of the summer, she will have earned a total of $630. She collected the same amount of money from each job. How much did each neighbor pay for her summer lawn service?

__$210__

If the mowing season lasts for 14 weeks, how much will Brianne earn for each job each week? __$15__

If she had worked for two more weeks, how much would she have earned? __$720__

Brianne agreed to shovel snow from the driveways and sidewalks for the same three neighbors. They agreed to pay her the same rate. However, it only snowed seven times that winter. How much did she earn shoveling snow? __$315__

What was her total income for both jobs? __$945__

Directions: Multiply or divide.

```
        623               940               815
12 ) 7,476     23 ) 21,620     40 ) 32,600
```

32 x 45 = __1,440__   28 x 15 = __420__   73 x 14 = __1,022__   92 x 30 = __2,760__

36

Review

Directions: Write the LCM of each pair of numbers.

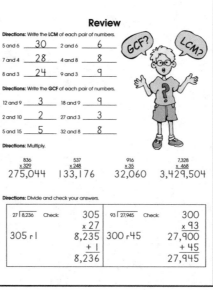

GCF?   LCM?

5 and 6 __30__   2 and 6 __6__

7 and 4 __28__   4 and 8 __8__

8 and 3 __24__   9 and 3 __9__

Directions: Write the GCF of each pair of numbers.

12 and 9 __3__   18 and 9 __9__

2 and 10 __2__   27 and 3 __3__

5 and 15 __5__   32 and 8 __8__

Directions: Multiply.

```
    836          537          916          7,328
  x 329        x 248         x 35         x  468
275,044      133,176       32,060      3,429,504
```

Directions: Divide and check your answers.

```
27 ) 8,236   Check:    305       93 ) 27,945   Check:     300
                      x 27                               x 93
  305 r 1            8,235       300 r 45              27,900
                    +   1                              +   45
                     8,236                             27,945
```

37

Adding and Subtracting Like Fractions

A **fraction** is a number that names part of a whole. Examples of fractions are $\frac{1}{2}$ and $\frac{1}{3}$. **Like fractions** have the same **denominator**, or bottom number. Examples of like fractions are $\frac{1}{4}$ and $\frac{3}{4}$.

To add or subtract fractions, the denominators must be the same. Add or subtract only the **numerators**, the numbers above the line in fractions.

Example:

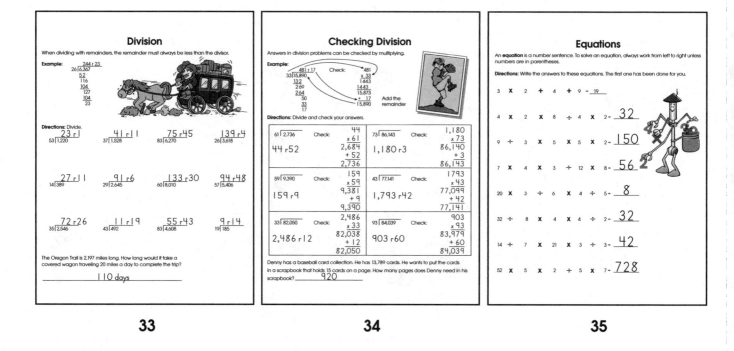

numerators
denominators
$\frac{5}{8} - \frac{1}{8} = \frac{4}{8}$

Directions: Add or subtract these fractions.

$\frac{6}{12} - \frac{3}{12} = \frac{3}{12}$ $\frac{4}{9} + \frac{1}{9} = \frac{5}{9}$ $\frac{1}{3} + \frac{1}{3} = \frac{2}{3}$ $\frac{5}{11} + \frac{4}{11} = \frac{9}{11}$

$\frac{3}{5} - \frac{1}{5} = \frac{2}{5}$ $\frac{5}{6} - \frac{2}{6} = \frac{3}{6}$ $\frac{3}{4} - \frac{2}{4} = \frac{1}{4}$ $\frac{5}{10} + \frac{3}{10} = \frac{8}{10}$

$\frac{3}{8} + \frac{2}{8} = \frac{5}{8}$ $\frac{1}{7} + \frac{4}{7} = \frac{5}{7}$ $\frac{2}{20} + \frac{15}{20} = \frac{17}{20}$ $\frac{11}{15} - \frac{9}{15} = \frac{2}{15}$

Directions: Color the part of each pizza that equals the given fraction.

$\frac{2}{4}$ + $\frac{1}{4}$ = $\frac{3}{4}$

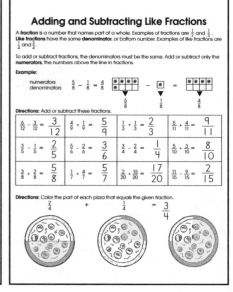

38

Adding and Subtracting Unlike Fractions

Unlike fractions have different denominators. Examples of unlike fractions are $\frac{1}{4}$ and $\frac{2}{5}$. To add or subtract fractions, the denominators must be the same.

Example:

Step 1: Make the denominators the same by finding the least common denominator. The LCD of a pair of fractions is the same as the least common multiple (LCM) of their denominators.

$\frac{1}{3} + \frac{1}{4} =$ Multiples of 3 are 3, 6, 9, **12**, 15.
Multiples of 4 are 4, 8, **12**, 16.
LCM (and LCD) = 12

Step 2: Multiply by a number that will give the LCD. The numerator and denominator must be multiplied by the same number.

A. $\frac{1}{3} \times \frac{4}{4} = \frac{4}{12}$ B. $\frac{1}{4} \times \frac{3}{3} = \frac{3}{12}$

Step 3: Add the fractions. $\frac{1}{3} + \frac{1}{4} = \frac{4}{12} + \frac{3}{12} = \frac{7}{12}$

Directions: Follow the above steps to add or subtract unlike fractions. Write the LCM.

$\frac{4}{4} + \frac{3}{8}$ $\frac{7}{8}$ LCM = 8	$\frac{3}{6} + \frac{1}{3}$ $\frac{5}{6}$ LCM = 6	$\frac{4}{5} - \frac{1}{4}$ $\frac{11}{20}$ LCM = 20
$\frac{2}{3} + \frac{2}{9}$ $\frac{8}{9}$ LCM = 9	$\frac{4}{7} - \frac{2}{14}$ $\frac{6}{14}$ LCM = 14	$\frac{7}{12} - \frac{2}{6}$ $\frac{1}{12}$ LCM = 12

The basketball team ordered two pizzas. They left $\frac{1}{3}$ of one and $\frac{1}{4}$ of the other. How much pizza was left? $\frac{7}{12}$

39

Reducing Fractions

A fraction is in lowest terms when the GCF of both the numerator and denominator is 1. These fractions are in lowest possible terms: $\frac{5}{6}$, $\frac{3}{8}$ and $\frac{29}{100}$.

Example: Write $\frac{4}{8}$ in lowest terms.

Step 1: Write the factors of 4 and 8.
Factors of 4 are **4**, 2, 1.
Factors of 8 are 1, 8, 2, **4**.
Step 2: Find the GCF: 4.
Step 3: Divide both the numerator and denominator by 4.

$$\frac{4}{8} \div \frac{4}{4} = \frac{1}{2}$$

Directions: Write each fraction in lowest terms.

$\frac{6}{8} = \frac{3}{4}$ lowest terms $\frac{9}{12} = \frac{3}{4}$ lowest terms

factors of 6: 6, 1, 2, 3 factors of 9: 1, 3, 9   3 GCF

factors of 8: 8, 1, 2, 4 factors of 12: 1, 2, 3, 4, 6, 12 4 GCF

$\frac{2}{6} = \frac{1}{3}$	$\frac{10}{15} = \frac{2}{3}$	$\frac{8}{32} = \frac{1}{4}$	$\frac{4}{10} = \frac{2}{5}$
$\frac{12}{18} = \frac{2}{3}$	$\frac{6}{8} = \frac{3}{4}$	$\frac{4}{6} = \frac{2}{3}$	$\frac{3}{9} = \frac{1}{3}$

Directions: Color the pizzas to show that $\frac{4}{6}$ in lowest terms is $\frac{2}{3}$.

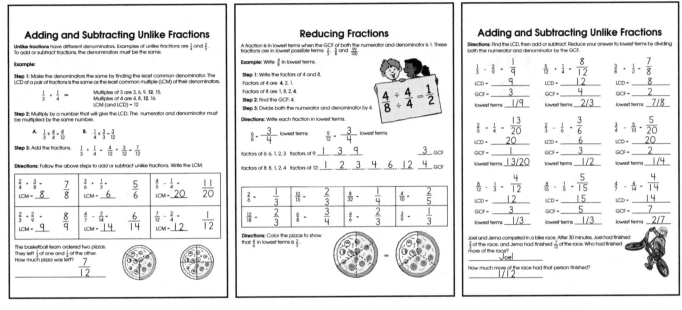

40

Adding and Subtracting Unlike Fractions

Directions: Find the LCD, then add or subtract. Reduce your answer to lowest terms by dividing both the numerator and denominator by the GCF.

$\frac{1}{3} - \frac{2}{9} = \frac{1}{9}$	$\frac{5}{12} + \frac{1}{4} = \frac{8}{12}$	$\frac{3}{8} + \frac{1}{2} = \frac{7}{8}$
LCD = 9 GCF = 3 lowest terms $\frac{1}{9}$	LCD = 12 GCF = 4 lowest terms $\frac{2}{3}$	LCD = 8 GCF = 2 lowest terms $\frac{7}{8}$
$\frac{2}{5} + \frac{1}{4} = \frac{13}{20}$	$\frac{2}{3} - \frac{1}{6} = \frac{3}{6}$	$\frac{3}{4} - \frac{5}{10} = \frac{5}{20}$
LCD = 20 GCF = 1 lowest terms $\frac{13}{20}$	LCD = 6 GCF = 3 lowest terms $\frac{1}{2}$	LCD = 20 GCF = 2 lowest terms $\frac{1}{4}$
$\frac{8}{12} - \frac{1}{3} = \frac{4}{12}$	$\frac{8}{15} - \frac{1}{5} = \frac{5}{15}$	$\frac{4}{7} - \frac{1}{14} = \frac{4}{14}$
LCD = 12 GCF = 3 lowest terms $\frac{1}{3}$	LCD = 15 GCF = 5 lowest terms $\frac{1}{3}$	LCD = 14 GCF = 7 lowest terms $\frac{2}{7}$

Joel and Jema competed in a bike race. After 30 minutes, Joel had finished $\frac{2}{3}$ of the race, and Jema had finished $\frac{7}{12}$ of the race. Who had finished more of the race? Joel

How much more of the race had that person finished? 1/12

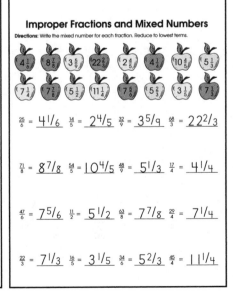

41

Improper Fractions

An **improper fraction** has a numerator that is greater than its denominator. An example of an improper fraction is $\frac{7}{6}$. An improper fraction should be reduced to its lowest terms.

Example: $\frac{5}{4}$ is an improper fraction because its numerator is greater than its denominator.

Step 1: Divide the numerator by the denominator: $5 \div 4 = 1$, r1
Step 2: Write the remainder as a fraction: $\frac{1}{4}$

$\frac{5}{4} = 1\frac{1}{4}$ $1\frac{1}{4}$ is a mixed number—a whole number and a fraction.

Directions: Follow the steps above to change the improper fractions to mixed numbers.

$\frac{9}{8} = 1\frac{1}{8}$	$\frac{11}{5} = 2\frac{1}{5}$	$\frac{5}{3} = 1\frac{2}{3}$	$\frac{7}{6} = 1\frac{1}{6}$	$\frac{8}{7} = 1\frac{1}{7}$	$\frac{4}{3} = 1\frac{1}{3}$
$\frac{21}{5} = 4\frac{1}{5}$	$\frac{9}{4} = 2\frac{1}{4}$	$\frac{3}{2} = 1\frac{1}{2}$	$\frac{12}{6} = 1\frac{1}{2}$	$\frac{25}{4} = 6\frac{1}{4}$	$\frac{8}{3} = 2\frac{2}{3}$

Sara had 29 duplicate stamps in her stamp collection. She decided to give them to four of her friends. If she gave each of them the same number of stamps, how many duplicates will she have left? $\frac{29}{4}$

Name the improper fraction in this problem. $\frac{29}{4}$

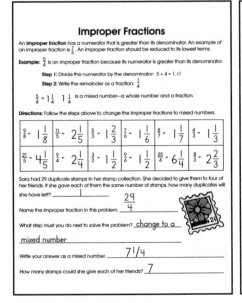

What step must you do next to solve the problem? change to a mixed number

Write your answer as a mixed number. 7 1/4

How many stamps could she give each of her friends? 7

42

Mixed Numbers

A **mixed number** is a whole number and a fraction together. An example of a mixed number is $2\frac{3}{4}$. A mixed number can be changed to an improper fraction.

Example: $2\frac{3}{4}$

Step 1: Multiply the denominator by the whole number: $4 \times 2 = 8$
Step 2: Add the numerator: $8 + 3 = 11$
Step 3: Write the sum over the denominator: $\frac{11}{4}$

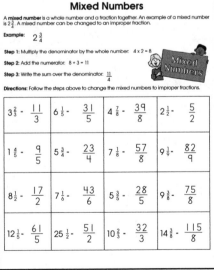

Directions: Follow the steps above to change the mixed numbers to improper fractions.

$3\frac{2}{3} = \frac{11}{3}$	$6\frac{1}{5} = \frac{31}{5}$	$4\frac{7}{8} = \frac{39}{8}$	$2\frac{1}{2} = \frac{5}{2}$
$1\frac{4}{5} = \frac{9}{5}$	$5\frac{3}{4} = \frac{23}{4}$	$7\frac{1}{8} = \frac{57}{8}$	$9\frac{1}{9} = \frac{82}{9}$
$8\frac{1}{2} = \frac{17}{2}$	$7\frac{1}{6} = \frac{43}{6}$	$5\frac{3}{5} = \frac{28}{5}$	$9\frac{3}{8} = \frac{75}{8}$
$12\frac{1}{5} = \frac{61}{5}$	$25\frac{1}{2} = \frac{51}{2}$	$10\frac{2}{3} = \frac{32}{3}$	$14\frac{3}{8} = \frac{115}{8}$

43

Improper Fractions and Mixed Numbers

Directions: Write the mixed number for each fraction. Reduce to lowest terms.

Apples: $4\frac{1}{3}$ $8\frac{7}{8}$ $3\frac{5}{6}$ $22\frac{2}{3}$ $2\frac{4}{5}$ $4\frac{1}{4}$ $10\frac{4}{5}$ $5\frac{1}{3}$

$7\frac{1}{4}$ $7\frac{7}{8}$ $5\frac{1}{2}$ $11\frac{1}{4}$ $7\frac{5}{6}$ $5\frac{2}{3}$ $3\frac{1}{5}$ $7\frac{1}{3}$

$\frac{26}{6} = 4\frac{1}{6}$ $\frac{14}{5} = 2\frac{4}{5}$ $\frac{32}{9} = 3\frac{5}{9}$ $\frac{68}{3} = 22\frac{2}{3}$

$\frac{71}{8} = 8\frac{7}{8}$ $\frac{54}{5} = 10\frac{4}{5}$ $\frac{48}{9} = 5\frac{1}{3}$ $\frac{17}{4} = 4\frac{1}{4}$

$\frac{47}{6} = 7\frac{5}{6}$ $\frac{11}{2} = 5\frac{1}{2}$ $\frac{63}{8} = 7\frac{7}{8}$ $\frac{29}{4} = 7\frac{1}{4}$

$\frac{22}{3} = 7\frac{1}{3}$ $\frac{16}{5} = 3\frac{1}{5}$ $\frac{34}{6} = 5\frac{2}{3}$ $\frac{45}{4} = 11\frac{1}{4}$

44

Adding Mixed Numbers

To add mixed numbers, first find the least common denominator.

Always reduce the answer to lowest terms.

Example:

$5\frac{1}{4} \rightarrow 5\frac{3}{12}$
$+6\frac{1}{3} \rightarrow +6\frac{4}{12}$
$11\frac{7}{12}$

Directions: Add. Reduce the answers to lowest terms.

$8\frac{1}{2}$ $5\frac{1}{4}$ $9\frac{3}{10}$ $8\frac{1}{5}$
$+7\frac{1}{4}$ $+2\frac{3}{8}$ $+7\frac{1}{5}$ $+6\frac{7}{10}$
$15\frac{3}{4}$ $7\frac{5}{8}$ $16\frac{1}{2}$ $14\frac{9}{10}$

$4\frac{4}{5}$ $3\frac{1}{4}$ $4\frac{1}{2}$ $6\frac{1}{12}$
$+3\frac{3}{10}$ $+7\frac{1}{2}$ $+1\frac{1}{3}$ $+3\frac{3}{4}$
$8\frac{1}{10}$ $10\frac{3}{4}$ $5\frac{5}{6}$ $9\frac{5}{6}$

$5\frac{1}{3}$ $6\frac{1}{3}$ $2\frac{2}{7}$ $3\frac{1}{2}$
$+2\frac{3}{9}$ $+2\frac{2}{5}$ $+4\frac{14}{14}$ $+3\frac{1}{4}$
$7\frac{2}{3}$ $8\frac{11}{15}$ $6\frac{5}{14}$ $6\frac{3}{4}$

The boys picked $3\frac{1}{2}$ baskets of apples. The girls picked $5\frac{1}{2}$ baskets. How many baskets of apples did the boys and girls pick in all? 9

45

Subtracting Mixed Numbers

To subtract mixed numbers, first find the least common denominator. Reduce the answer to its lowest terms.

Directions: Subtract. Reduce to lowest terms.

Example:

$6\frac{5}{8} \rightarrow 6\frac{10}{16}$
$-3\frac{4}{16} \rightarrow -3\frac{4}{16}$
$3\frac{6}{16} = 3\frac{3}{8}$

$2\frac{3}{7}$ $7\frac{2}{3}$ $6\frac{3}{4}$ $9\frac{5}{12}$
$-1\frac{1}{14}$ $-5\frac{1}{8}$ $-2\frac{3}{8}$ $-5\frac{9}{24}$
$1\frac{5}{14}$ $2\frac{13}{24}$ $4\frac{1}{2}$ $4\frac{1}{24}$

$5\frac{1}{2}$ $7\frac{3}{8}$ $8\frac{3}{8}$ $11\frac{5}{8}$
$-3\frac{1}{3}$ $-5\frac{1}{6}$ $-6\frac{1}{12}$ $-7\frac{1}{2}$
$2\frac{1}{6}$ $2\frac{5}{24}$ $1\frac{23}{24}$ $4\frac{3}{4}$

$9\frac{3}{5}$ $4\frac{4}{5}$ $9\frac{2}{3}$ $14\frac{3}{8}$
$-7\frac{1}{15}$ $-2\frac{1}{4}$ $-4\frac{1}{6}$ $-9\frac{3}{16}$
$2\frac{8}{15}$ $2\frac{11}{24}$ $5\frac{1}{2}$ $5\frac{3}{16}$

The Rodriguez Farm has $9\frac{1}{2}$ acres of corn. The Johnson Farm has $7\frac{1}{3}$ acres of corn. How many more acres of corn does the Rodriguez Farm have? $2\frac{1}{6}$

46

Review

Directions: Match.

$\frac{1}{4} + \frac{1}{3}$ — $\frac{19}{8}$
$\frac{1}{5} - \frac{1}{6}$ — $\frac{7}{5}$
$1\frac{1}{6}$ — $\frac{1}{30}$
$1\frac{2}{5}$ — $\frac{7}{12}$
$2\frac{3}{8}$ — $\frac{7}{6}$

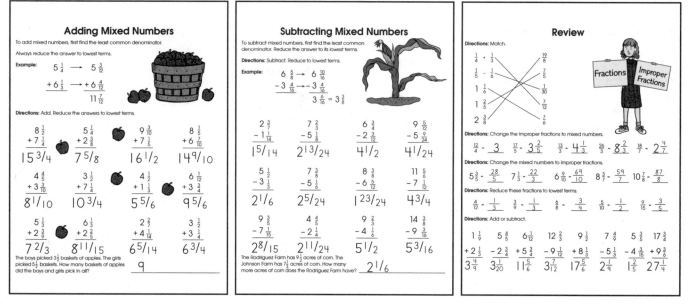

Directions: Change the improper fractions to mixed numbers.

$\frac{12}{4} = 3$ $\frac{17}{5} = 3\frac{2}{5}$ $\frac{13}{3} = 4\frac{1}{3}$ $\frac{26}{3} = 8\frac{2}{3}$ $\frac{18}{7} = 2\frac{4}{7}$

Directions: Change the mixed numbers to improper fractions.

$5\frac{3}{5} = \frac{28}{5}$ $7\frac{1}{3} = \frac{22}{3}$ $6\frac{9}{10} = \frac{69}{10}$ $8\frac{3}{7} = \frac{59}{7}$ $10\frac{7}{8} = \frac{87}{8}$

Directions: Reduce these fractions to lowest terms.

$\frac{4}{12} = \frac{1}{3}$ $\frac{3}{9} = \frac{1}{3}$ $\frac{6}{8} = \frac{3}{4}$ $\frac{5}{10} = \frac{1}{2}$ $\frac{9}{15} = \frac{3}{5}$

Directions: Add or subtract.

$1\frac{1}{9}$ $5\frac{4}{5}$ $6\frac{1}{12}$ $12\frac{2}{3}$ $9\frac{1}{2}$ $7\frac{4}{9}$ $5\frac{3}{5}$ $17\frac{3}{4}$
$+2\frac{1}{3}$ $-2\frac{3}{4}$ $+5\frac{3}{4}$ $-9\frac{1}{12}$ $+8\frac{1}{3}$ $-5\frac{1}{3}$ $-4\frac{3}{15}$ $+9\frac{1}{2}$
$3\frac{4}{9}$ $3\frac{1}{20}$ $11\frac{5}{6}$ $3\frac{7}{12}$ $17\frac{5}{6}$ $2\frac{1}{9}$ $1\frac{2}{5}$ $27\frac{1}{4}$

47

Comparing Fractions

Directions: Use the symbol > (greater than), < (less than) or = (equal to) to show the relationship between each pair of fractions.

$\frac{1}{2} > \frac{1}{3}$ $\frac{2}{5} < \frac{3}{7}$ $\frac{3}{8} < \frac{2}{4}$

$\frac{3}{4} = \frac{6}{8}$ $\frac{2}{3} < \frac{4}{5}$ $\frac{3}{9} = \frac{1}{3}$

$\frac{3}{12} = \frac{1}{4}$ $\frac{2}{14} = \frac{1}{7}$ $\frac{5}{15} < \frac{2}{3}$

If Kelly gave $\frac{1}{3}$ of a pizza to Holly and $\frac{1}{5}$ to Diane, how much did she have left? $\frac{7}{15}$

Holly decided to share $\frac{1}{2}$ of her share of the pizza with Deb. How much did each of them actually get? $\frac{1}{6}$

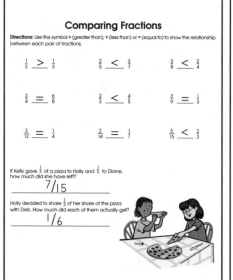

48

Ordering Fractions

When putting fractions in order from smallest to largest or largest to smallest, it helps to find a common denominator first.

Example:

$\frac{1}{3}, \frac{1}{2}$ changed to $\frac{2}{6}, \frac{3}{6}$

Directions: Put the following fractions in order from least to largest value.

			Least			Largest
$\frac{1}{2}$	$\frac{2}{7}$	$\frac{4}{5}$	$\frac{1}{3}$	$2/7$	$1/3$	$1/2$	$4/5$
$\frac{3}{12}$	$\frac{3}{6}$	$\frac{1}{3}$	$\frac{3}{4}$	$3/12$	$1/3$	$3/6$	$3/4$
$\frac{2}{5}$	$\frac{4}{15}$	$\frac{3}{5}$	$\frac{5}{15}$	$4/15$	$5/15$	$2/5$	$3/5$
$3\frac{4}{5}$	$3\frac{2}{5}$	$\frac{9}{5}$	$3\frac{1}{5}$	$9/5$	$3\,1/5$	$3\,2/5$	$3\,4/5$
$9\frac{1}{3}$	$9\frac{2}{3}$	$9\frac{9}{12}$	$8\frac{2}{3}$	$8\,2/3$	$9\,1/3$	$9\,2/3$	$9\,9/12$
$5\frac{8}{12}$	$5\frac{5}{12}$	$5\frac{4}{24}$	$5\frac{3}{6}$	$5\,4/24$	$5\,5/12$	$5\,3/6$	$5\,8/12$
$4\frac{3}{5}$	$5\frac{7}{15}$	$6\frac{2}{5}$	$5\frac{1}{5}$	$4\,3/5$	$5\,1/5$	$5\,7/15$	$6\,2/5$

Four dogs were selected as finalists at a dog show. They were judged in four separate categories. One received a perfect score in each area. The dog with a score closest to four is the winner. Their scores are listed below. Which dog won the contest? Dog A

Dog A ($3\frac{4}{5}$) Dog B $3\frac{2}{3}$ Dog C $3\frac{5}{15}$ Dog D $3\frac{9}{12}$

49

Multiplying Fractions

To multiply fractions, follow these steps:

$\frac{1}{2} \times \frac{3}{4} =$ **Step 1:** Multiply the numerators. $1 \times 3 = 3$
Step 2: Multiply the denominators. $2 \times 4 = 8$

When multiplying a fraction by a whole number, first change the whole number to a fraction.

Example:

$\frac{1}{2} \times 8 = \frac{1}{2} \times \frac{8}{1} = \frac{8}{2} = 4$ reduced to lowest terms

Directions: Multiply. Reduce your answers to lowest terms.

$\frac{3}{4} \times \frac{1}{6} = \frac{1}{8}$	$\frac{1}{2} \times \frac{5}{8} = \frac{5}{16}$	$\frac{2}{3} \times \frac{1}{6} = \frac{1}{9}$	$\frac{2}{3} \times \frac{1}{2} = \frac{1}{3}$
$\frac{5}{6} \times 4 = 3\frac{1}{3}$	$\frac{3}{8} \times \frac{1}{16} = \frac{3}{128}$	$\frac{1}{5} \times 5 = 1$	$\frac{7}{8} \times \frac{3}{4} = \frac{21}{32}$
$\frac{7}{11} \times \frac{1}{3} = \frac{7}{33}$	$\frac{2}{9} \times \frac{9}{4} = \frac{1}{2}$	$\frac{1}{3} \times \frac{1}{3} \times \frac{1}{3} = \frac{1}{27}$	$\frac{1}{8} \times \frac{1}{4} \times \frac{1}{2} = \frac{1}{64}$

Jennifer has 10 pets. Two-fifths of the pets are cats, one-half are fish and one-tenth are dogs. How many of each pet does she have?

Cats = 4
Fish = 5
Dogs = 1

50

Multiplying Mixed Numbers

Multiply mixed numbers by first changing them to improper fractions. Always reduce your answers to lowest terms.

Example:

$2\frac{1}{3} \times 1\frac{1}{8} = \frac{7}{3} \times \frac{9}{8} = \frac{63}{24} = 2\frac{15}{24} = 2\frac{5}{8}$

Directions: Multiply. Reduce to lowest terms.

$4\frac{1}{4} \times 2\frac{1}{5} = 9\frac{7}{20}$	$1\frac{1}{3} \times 3\frac{1}{4} = 4\frac{1}{3}$	$1\frac{1}{9} \times 3\frac{3}{5} = 4$
$1\frac{6}{7} \times 4\frac{1}{2} = 8\frac{5}{14}$	$2\frac{3}{4} \times 2\frac{3}{5} = 7\frac{3}{20}$	$4\frac{2}{3} \times 3\frac{1}{7} = 14\frac{2}{3}$
$6\frac{2}{3} \times 2\frac{1}{8} = 13\frac{3}{5}$	$3\frac{1}{7} \times 4\frac{5}{8} = 14\frac{15}{28}$	$7\frac{3}{8} \times 2\frac{1}{9} = 15\frac{41}{72}$

Sunnyside Farm has two barns with 25 stalls in each barn. Cows use $\frac{3}{5}$ of the stalls, and horses use the rest.

How many stalls are for cows? ___30___

How many are for horses? ___20___

(Hint: First, find how many total stalls are in the two barns.)

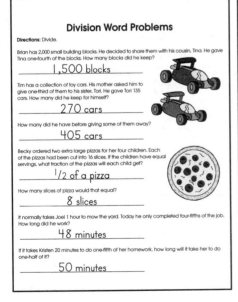

51

Dividing Fractions

To divide fractions, follow these steps:

$\frac{3}{4} \div \frac{1}{4} =$

Step 1: "Invert" the divisor. That means to turn it upside down.

$\frac{3}{4} \qquad \frac{4}{1}$

Step 2: Multiply the two fractions:

$\frac{3}{4} \times \frac{4}{1} = \frac{12}{4}$

Step 3: Reduce the fraction to lowest terms by dividing the denominator into the numerator.

$12 \div 4 = 3$
$\frac{3}{4} \div \frac{1}{4} = 3$

Directions: Follow the above steps to divide fractions.

$\frac{1}{4} \div \frac{1}{5} = 1\frac{1}{4}$	$\frac{1}{3} \div \frac{1}{12} = 4$	$\frac{3}{4} \div \frac{1}{3} = 2\frac{1}{4}$
$\frac{5}{12} \div \frac{1}{3} = 1\frac{1}{4}$	$\frac{3}{4} \div \frac{1}{6} = 4\frac{1}{2}$	$\frac{2}{9} \div \frac{2}{3} = \frac{1}{3}$
$\frac{5}{7} \div \frac{1}{2} = 1\frac{5}{7}$	$\frac{2}{3} \div \frac{4}{6} = 1$	$\frac{1}{8} \div \frac{2}{3} = \frac{3}{16}$
$\frac{4}{5} \div \frac{1}{3} = 2\frac{2}{5}$	$\frac{4}{8} \div \frac{1}{2} = 1$	$\frac{5}{12} \div \frac{6}{8} = \frac{5}{9}$

52

Dividing Whole Numbers by Fractions

Follow these steps to divide a whole number by a fraction:

$8 \div \frac{1}{4} =$

Step 1: Write the whole number as a fraction:

$\frac{8}{1} \div \frac{1}{4} =$

Step 2: Invert the divisor.

$\frac{8}{1} \qquad \frac{4}{1} =$

Step 3: Multiply the two fractions:

$\frac{8}{1} \times \frac{4}{1} = \frac{32}{1}$

Step 4: Reduce the fraction to lowest terms by dividing the denominator into the numerator: $32 \div 1 = 32$

Directions: Follow the above steps to divide a whole number by a fraction.

$6 \div \frac{1}{3} = 18$	$4 \div \frac{1}{2} = 8$	$21 \div \frac{1}{3} = 63$
$8 \div \frac{1}{2} = 16$	$3 \div \frac{1}{6} = 18$	$15 \div \frac{1}{7} = 105$
$9 \div \frac{1}{5} = 45$	$4 \div \frac{1}{9} = 36$	$12 \div \frac{1}{6} = 72$

Three-fourths of a bag of popcorn fits into one bowl. How many bowls do you need if you have six bags of popcorn? ___8___

53

Division Word Problems

Directions: Divide.

Brian has 2,000 small building blocks. He decided to share them with his cousin, Tina. He gave Tina one-fourth of the blocks. How many blocks did he keep?

___1,500 blocks___

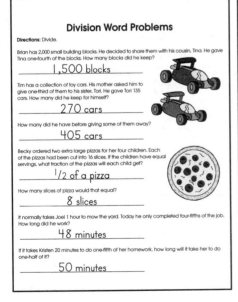

Tim has a collection of toy cars. His mother asked him to give one-third of them to his sister, Tori. He gave Tori 135 cars. How many did he keep for himself?

___270 cars___

How many did he have before giving some of them away?

___405 cars___

Becky ordered two extra large pizzas for her four children. Each of the pizzas had been cut into 16 slices. If the children have equal servings, what fraction of the pizzas will each child get?

___1/2 of a pizza___

How many slices of pizza would that equal?

___8 slices___

It normally takes Joel 1 hour to mow the yard. Today he only completed four-fifths of the job. How long did he work?

___48 minutes___

If it takes Kristen 20 minutes to do one-fifth of her homework, how long will it take her to do one-half of it?

___50 minutes___

54

Decimals

A **decimal** is a number with one or more places to the right of a decimal point.

Examples: 6.5 and 2.25

Fractions with denominators of 10 or 100 can be written as decimals.

Examples:

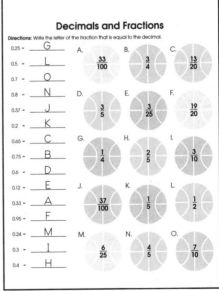

$\frac{7}{10} = 0.7$

0	.	7	0
ones		tenths	hundredths

$1\frac{52}{100} = 1.52$

1	.	5	2
ones		tenths	hundredths

Directions: Write the fractions as decimals.

$\frac{1}{2} = \frac{}{10} = 0.\underline{5}$

$\frac{2}{5} = \frac{}{10} = 0.\underline{4}$

$\frac{1}{5} = \frac{}{10} = 0.\underline{2}$

$\frac{3}{5} = \frac{}{10} = 0.\underline{6}$

		1/10
	$\frac{1}{4}$	$\frac{1}{5}$ 1/10
$\frac{1}{2}$	$\frac{1}{4}$	$\frac{1}{5}$ 1/10
	$\frac{1}{4}$	$\frac{1}{5}$ 1/10
$\frac{1}{2}$	$\frac{1}{4}$	$\frac{1}{5}$ 1/10

$\frac{63}{100} = 0.63$	$2\frac{8}{10} = 2.8$	$38\frac{4}{100} = 38.04$	$6\frac{13}{100} = 6.13$
$\frac{1}{4} = 0.25$	$\frac{2}{5} = 0.4$	$\frac{1}{50} = 0.02$	$\frac{100}{200} = 0.5$
$5\frac{2}{100} = 5.02$	$\frac{4}{25} = 0.16$	$15\frac{3}{5} = 15.6$	$\frac{3}{100} = 0.03$

55

Decimals and Fractions

Directions: Write the letter of the fraction that is equal to the decimal.

0.25 = ___G___
0.5 = ___L___
0.7 = ___O___
0.8 = ___N___
0.37 = ___J___
0.2 = ___K___
0.65 = ___C___
0.75 = ___B___
0.6 = ___D___
0.12 = ___E___
0.33 = ___A___
0.95 = ___F___
0.24 = ___M___
0.3 = ___I___
0.4 = ___H___

A. $\frac{33}{100}$	B. $\frac{3}{4}$	C. $\frac{13}{20}$
D. $\frac{3}{5}$	E. $\frac{3}{25}$	F. $\frac{19}{20}$
G. $\frac{1}{4}$	H. $\frac{2}{5}$	I. $\frac{3}{10}$
J. $\frac{37}{100}$	K. $\frac{1}{5}$	L. $\frac{1}{2}$
M. $\frac{6}{25}$	N. $\frac{4}{5}$	O. $\frac{7}{10}$

56

Adding and Subtracting Decimals

A decimal is another way of writing a fraction. Decimals and fractions are numbers less than one.

Directions: Add or subtract. Remember to keep the decimal point in the proper place.

0.5 + 0.8 **1.3**	0.35 + 0.25 **0.60**	47.5 - 32.7 **14.8**	85.7 - 9.8 **75.9**
13.90 + 4.23 **18.13**	9.53 - 8.16 **1.37**	72.8 - 63.9 **8.9**	6.43 + 4.58 **11.01**
638.07 - 19.34 **618.73**	811.060 + 78.430 **889.490**	521.09 - 148.75 **372.34**	
916.635 + 172.136 **1,088.771**	287.768 - 63.951 **223.817**	467.05 - 398.19 **68.86**	

Sean ran a 1-mile race in 5.58 minutes. Carlos ran it in 6.38 minutes. How much faster did Sean run?

0.8 minutes

57

Multiplying Decimals

Multiply with decimals the same way you do with whole numbers. The decimal point moves in multiplication. Count the number of decimals in the problem and use the same number of decimals in your answer.

Example:
3.5
x 1.5
1 7 5
3 5
5.2 5

Directions: Multiply.

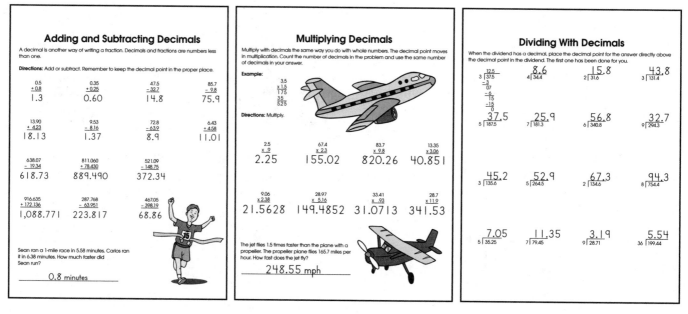

2.5 x .9 **2.25**	67.4 x 2.3 **155.02**	83.7 x 9.8 **820.26**	13.35 x 3.06 **40.851**
9.06 x 2.38 **21.5628**	28.97 x 5.16 **149.4852**	33.41 x .93 **31.0713**	28.7 x 11.9 **341.53**

The jet flies 1.5 times faster than the plane with a propeller. The propeller plane flies 165.7 miles per hour. How fast does the jet fly?

248.55 mph

58

Dividing With Decimals

When the dividend has a decimal, place the decimal point for the answer directly above the decimal point in the dividend. The first one has been done for you.

12.5 3) 37.5 - 3 - 6 15 - 15 0	8.6 4) 34.4	15.8 2) 31.6	43.8 3) 131.4
37.5 5) 187.5	25.9 7) 181.3	56.8 6) 340.8	32.7 9) 294.3
45.2 3) 135.6	52.9 5) 264.5	67.3 2) 134.6	94.3 8) 754.4
7.05 5) 35.25	11.35 7) 79.45	3.19 9) 28.71	5.54 36) 199.44

59

Dividing Decimals by Decimals

When the divisor has a decimal, you must eliminate it before dividing. You can do this by moving it to the right to create a whole number. You must also move the decimal the same number of spaces to the right in the dividend.

Sometimes you need to add zeros to do this.

Example:
0.25) 85.50   changes to   342
25) 8550
- 75
105
- 100
50
- 50
0

Directions: Divide.

93 0.3) 27.9	71 0.6) 42.6	91 0.9) 81.9	119 0.7) 83.3
58 0.4) 23.2	81 0.7) 56.7	9 1.2) 10.8	63 2.2) 138.6
450 12.6) 5,670	120 4.7) 564	98 8.6) 842.8	543 3.7) 2,009.1
325 5.9) 1,917.5	320 4.3) 1,376	318 2.9) 922.2	2079 2.7) 5613.3

60

Review

Directions: Multiply. Reduce to lowest terms.

$\frac{1}{4} \times \frac{1}{5} = \frac{1}{20}$	$\frac{5}{8} \times \frac{3}{10} = \frac{3}{16}$	$\frac{2}{9} \times \frac{3}{4} = \frac{1}{6}$	$\frac{5}{12} \times \frac{8}{15} = \frac{2}{9}$
$5\frac{1}{4} \times 3\frac{1}{5} = 16\frac{4}{5}$	$3\frac{3}{4} \times 2\frac{1}{7} = 8\frac{1}{28}$	$4\frac{1}{6} \times 3\frac{3}{5} = 15$	$6\frac{3}{8} \times 1\frac{1}{9} = 7\frac{1}{12}$

Directions: Divide. Reduce to lowest terms.

$5 \div \frac{1}{5} = 25$	$18 \div \frac{1}{9} = 162$	$8 \div \frac{1}{3} = 24$
$18 \div \frac{1}{4} = 72$	$63 \div \frac{5}{8} = 100\frac{4}{5}$	$42 \div \frac{1}{5} = 210$

Directions: Write these fractions as decimals.

$\frac{7}{100} = $ **0.07** $\frac{2}{5} = $ **0.4** $37\frac{3}{10} = $ **37.3** $\frac{5}{100} = $ **0.05**

Directions: Add or subtract.

14.5 + 3.8 **18.3**	26.93 - 18.45 **8.48**	137.092 - 98.135 **38.957**	291.036 + 187.984 **479.020**

Directions: Multiply.

83.3 x 0.6 **49.98**	42.91 x 2.03 **87.1073**	12.3 x 0.7 **8.61**	27.09 x 3.16 **85.6044**

61

Geometry

Geometry is the branch of mathematics that has to do with points, lines and shapes.

Directions: Use the Glossary on pages 105 and 106 if you need help. Write the word from the box that is described below.

triangle	square	cube	angle
line	ray	segment	rectangle

a collection of points that goes on and on in opposite directions	**line**
a figure with three sides and three corners	**triangle**
a figure with four equal sides and four corners	**square**
part of a line that has one end point and goes on and on in one direction	**ray**
part of a line having two end points	**segment**
a space figure with six square faces	**cube**
two rays with a common end point	**angle**
a figure with four corners and four sides	**rectangle**

62

Geometry

Review the definitions on the previous page before completing the problems below.

Directions: Identify the labeled section of each of the following diagrams.

AB = _segment_

ABC = _angle_

AB = _segment_

CD = _line_

AC = _ray_

AB = _segment_

EBC = _angle_

BC = _ray_

Similar, Congruent and Symmetrical Figures

Similar figures have the same shape but have varying sizes.

Figures that are **congruent** have identical shapes but different orientations. That means they face in different directions.

Symmetrical figures can be divided equally into two identical parts.

Directions: Cross out the shape that does not belong in each group. Label the two remaining shapes as similar, congruent or symmetrical.

congruent

congruent

similar

symmetrical

Perimeter and Area

The **perimeter (P)** of a figure is the distance around it. To find the perimeter, add the lengths of the sides.

The **area (A)** of a figure is the number of units in a figure. Find the area by multiplying the length of a figure by its width.

Example:

P = 16 units
A = 16 units

Directions: Find the perimeter and area of each figure.

P = _16 units_
A = _13 units_

P = _12 units_
A = _6 units_

9 Yards

9 Yards
P = _36 yards_
A = _81 sq. yards_

2 Miles

45 Miles
P = _94 miles_
A = _90 sq. miles_

63 **64** **65**

Volume

The **volume** of a figure is the number of cubic units inside it.

Example: Volume = 6 cubic units

Directions: Draw figures to show the volumes given. Use the dot pattern to help you. The first one has been done for you.

1 cubic unit

3 cubic units

5 cubic units

6 cubic units

7 cubic units

Volume

The formula for finding the volume of a box is length times width times height (**L x W x H**). The answer is given in cubic units.

Directions: Solve the problems.

Example:

Height 8 ft.
Length 8 ft.
Width 8 ft. **L x W x H = volume**
8' x 8' x 8' = 512 cubic ft. or 512 ft.³

Height 8 ft.
Length 8 ft.
Width 8 ft.

4 ft. 12 ft. 6 ft.
V = _288ft._³

Height 8 ft.
6 ft. 2 ft.
1.5 ft.
V = _18ft._³

7 ft. 9 ft.
3 ft.
V = _189ft._³

2 ft.
2 ft. 2 ft.
V = _8ft._³

3 ft. 20 ft.
6 ft.
V = _360ft._³

5 in. 22 in.
15 in.
V = _1650_ in.³

V = _137.5_ ft.³

Perimeter and Area

Directions: Use the formulas for finding perimeter and area to solve these problems.

Julie's family moved to a new house. Her parents said she could have the largest bedroom. Julie knew she would need to find the perimeter of each room to find which one was largest.

One rectangular bedroom is 7 feet wide and 12 feet long. Another is 11 feet long and 9 feet wide. The third bedroom is a square. It is 9 feet wide and 9 feet long. Which one should she select to have the largest room?

the 11 x 9 room

The new home also has a swimming pool in the backyard. It is 32 feet long and 18 feet wide. What is the perimeter of the pool?

_100 ft._

Julie's mother wants to plant flowers on each side of the new house. She will need three plants for every foot of space. The house is 75 feet across the front and back and 37.5 feet along each side. Find the perimeter of the house.

_225 ft._

How many plants should she buy? _675 plants_

The family decided to buy new carpeting for several rooms. Complete the necessary information to determine how much carpeting to buy.

Den: 12 ft. x 14 ft. = _168_ sq. ft.

Master Bedroom: 20 ft. x _18ft._ = 360 sq. ft.

Family Room: _15ft._ x 25 ft. = 375 sq. ft.

Total square feet of carpeting: _903 sq. ft._

66 **67** **68**

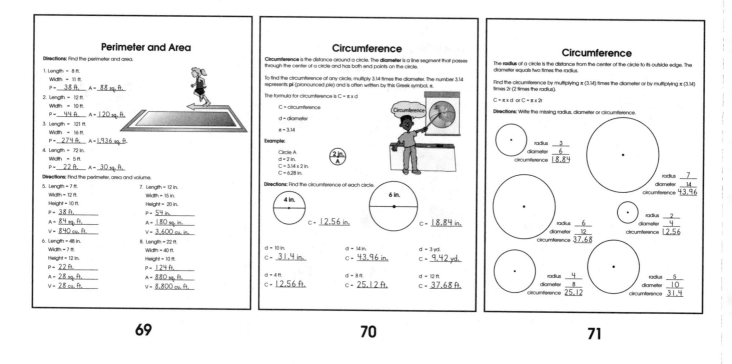

Perimeter and Area

Directions: Find the perimeter and area.

1. Length = 8 ft.
   Width = 11 ft.
   P = _38 ft._   A = _88 sq. ft._

2. Length = 12 ft.
   Width = 10 ft.
   P = _44 ft._   A = _120 sq. ft._

3. Length = 121 ft.
   Width = 16 ft.
   P = _274 ft._   A = _1,936 sq. ft._

4. Length = 72 ft.
   Width = 5 ft.
   P = _22 ft._   A = _30 sq. ft._

Directions: Find the perimeter, area and volume.

5. Length = 7 ft.
   Width = 12 ft.
   Height = 10 ft.
   P = _38 ft._
   A = _84 sq. ft._
   V = _840 cu. ft._

6. Length = 48 in.
   Width = 7 ft.
   Height = 12 in.
   P = _22 ft._
   A = _28 sq. ft._
   V = _28 cu. ft._

7. Length = 12 in.
   Width = 15 in.
   Height = 20 in.
   P = _54 in._
   A = _180 sq. in._
   V = _3,600 cu. in._

8. Length = 22 ft.
   Width = 40 ft.
   Height = 10 ft.
   P = _124 ft._
   A = _880 sq. ft._
   V = _8,800 cu. ft._

69

Circumference

Circumference is the distance around a circle. The **diameter** is a line segment that passes through the center of a circle and has both end points on the circle.

To find the circumference of any circle, multiply 3.14 times the diameter. The number 3.14 represents **pi** (pronounced pie) and is often written by this Greek symbol, π.

The formula for circumference is C = π x d

C = circumference
d = diameter
π = 3.14

Example:

Circle A
d = 2 in.
C = 3.14 x 2 in.
C = 6.28 in.

Directions: Find the circumference of each circle.

4 in. — C = _12.56 in._
6 in. — C = _18.84 in._

d = 10 in. — C = _31.4 in._
d = 14 in. — C = _43.96 in._
d = 3 yd. — C = _9.42 yd._

d = 4 ft. — C = _12.56 ft._
d = 8 ft. — C = _25.12 ft._
d = 12 ft. — C = _37.68 ft._

70

Circumference

The **radius** of a circle is the distance from the center of the circle to its outside edge. The diameter equals two times the radius.

Find the circumference by multiplying π (3.14) times the diameter or by multiplying π (3.14) times 2r (2 times the radius).

C = π x d or C = π x 2r

Directions: Write the missing radius, diameter or circumference.

radius _3_
diameter _6_
circumference _18.84_

radius _7_
diameter _14_
circumference _43.96_

radius _6_
diameter _12_
circumference _37.68_

radius _2_
diameter _4_
circumference _12.56_

radius _4_
diameter _8_
circumference _25.12_

radius _5_
diameter _10_
circumference _31.4_

71

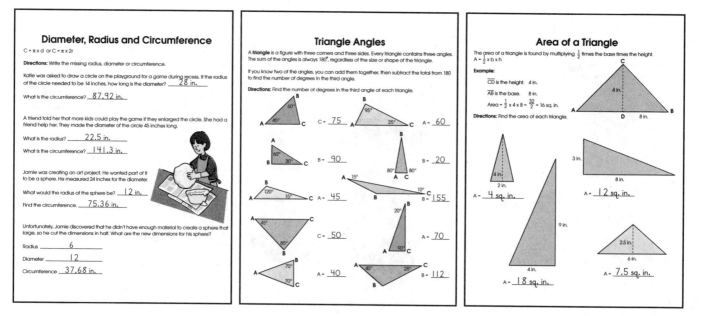

Diameter, Radius and Circumference

C = π x d or C = π x 2r

Directions: Write the missing radius, diameter or circumference.

Katie was asked to draw a circle on the playground for a game during recess. If the radius of the circle needed to be 14 inches, how long is the diameter? _28 in._

What is the circumference? _87.92 in._

A friend told her that more kids could play the game if they enlarged the circle. She had a friend help her. They made the diameter of the circle 45 inches long.

What is the radius? _22.5 in._

What is the circumference? _141.3 in._

Jamie was creating an art project. He wanted part of it to be a sphere. He measured 24 inches for the diameter.

What would the radius of the sphere be? _12 in._

Find the circumference. _75.36 in._

Unfortunately, Jamie discovered that he didn't have enough material to create a sphere that large, so he cut the dimensions in half. What are the new dimensions for his sphere?

Radius _6_

Diameter _12_

Circumference _37.68 in._

72

Triangle Angles

A **triangle** is a figure with three corners and three sides. Every triangle contains three angles. The sum of the angles is always 180°, regardless of the size or shape of the triangle.

If you know two of the angles, you can add them together, then subtract the total from 180 to find the number of degrees in the third angle.

Directions: Find the number of degrees in the third angle of each triangle.

C = _75_
A = _60_
B = _90_
B = _20_
A = _45_
B = _155_
C = _50_
A = _70_
A = _40_
B = _112_

73

Area of a Triangle

The area of a triangle is found by multiplying ½ times the base times the height.
A = ½ x b x h

Example:

$\overline{CD}$ is the height. 4 in.
$\overline{AB}$ is the base. 8 in.
Area = ½ x 4 x 8 = $\frac{32}{2}$ = 16 sq. in.

Directions: Find the area of each triangle.

A = _4 sq. in._
A = _12 sq. in._
A = _18 sq. in._
A = _7.5 sq. in._

74

Estimating Area

Estimating area means giving an approximate number of square units in a figure.

Example: The Andrews family is building a swimming pool. To find out how much material they will need, they must estimate the area of the pool.

Step 2: Count the number of partial squares: 12
Step 3: Divide the number of partial squares by 2: 6
Step 4: Add ½ the number of the partial squares to the number of whole squares. Round to the nearest whole number.

14 + 6 = 20

Directions: Follow the steps to estimate the area of each figure. Round the answer to the nearest whole number.

whole units 21
partial units 4
A = __23__ sq. units

whole units 17
partial units 4
A = __19__ sq. units

Answers may vary slightly

whole units __59__
partial units __24__
A = __71__ sq. units

75

Space Figures

Space figures are figures whose points are in more than one plane. Cubes and cylinders are space figures.

rectangular prism   cone   cube   cylinder   sphere   pyramid

A **prism** has two identical, parallel bases.

All of the faces on a **rectangular prism** are rectangles.

A **cube** is a prism with six identical, square faces.

A **pyramid** is a space figure whose base is a polygon and whose faces are triangles with a common vertex—the point where two rays meet.

A **cylinder** has a curved surface and two parallel bases that are identical circles.

A **cone** has one circular, flat face and one vertex.

A **sphere** has no flat surface. All points are an equal distance from the center.

Directions: Circle the name of the figure you see in each of these familiar objects

cone   (sphere)   cylinder

cone   sphere   (cylinder)

cube   (rectangular prism)   pyramid

(cone)   pyramid   cylinder

76

Review

Directions: Find the perimeter and area of each figure.

P = __36 in.__
A = __80 sq. in.__

P = __24 in.__
A = __36 sq. in.__

Directions: Find the circumference of each circle.

D = 3 in.
C = __9.42 in.__

D = 5 ft.
C = __15.7 ft.__

D = 6 yd.
C = __18.84 yd.__

Directions: Find the area of each triangle.

A = __40 sq. in.__

A = __35 sq. in.__

Directions: Draw a line from the space figure to its name.

cone
pyramid
cylinder
cube

77

Measurement

Directions: Use the map to help plan a day at the zoo.

City Zoo

KEY
A ENTRANCE
B REPTILES
C ELEPHANTS
D SEALS
E LIONS
F MONKEYS
G BIRDS
H FOOD CENTER

The class is going to the zoo. They want to see the elephants, monkeys, lions and birds before lunch at the food center. What is a logical path to travel from A to H to see the animals?

A → __F__ → __C__ G → H

What path would you take to see the seals, reptiles and monkeys before leaving the zoo?

H → B → A → F → D → A

78

Measurement

Directions: Use the map on the previous page to answer these questions.

What is the shortest path to follow from the front gate in order to see the elephants, monkeys and birds?

A → F → G → C

Traveling from the food center, which animal arena is farthest away? __seals__

Which is closest? __reptiles__

Which animals would you see if you only traveled the path on the perimeter of the zoo?

seals, elephants, reptiles

What shape would you create if you followed the path from A to D to F and back to A?

triangle

Is it possible to create a square by following any of the paths? If so, which ones?

no

79

Length

Inches, feet, yards and **miles** are used to measure length in the United States.

12 inches = 1 foot (ft.)
3 feet = 1 yard (yd.)
36 inches = 1 yard
1,760 yards = 1 mile (mi.)

Directions: Circle the best unit to measure each object. The first one has been done for you.

the length of a   (inches)   feet   yards   miles

the height of a   inches   (feet)   yards   miles

the length of a   (inches)   feet   yards   miles

distance to the   inches   feet   yards   (miles)

the height of a   inches   (feet)   (yards)   miles

the length of a   field   inches   (feet)   (yards)   miles

80

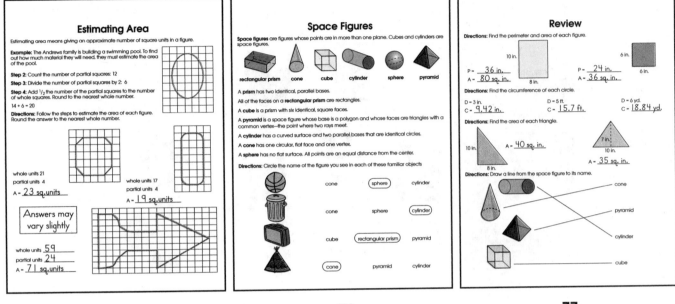
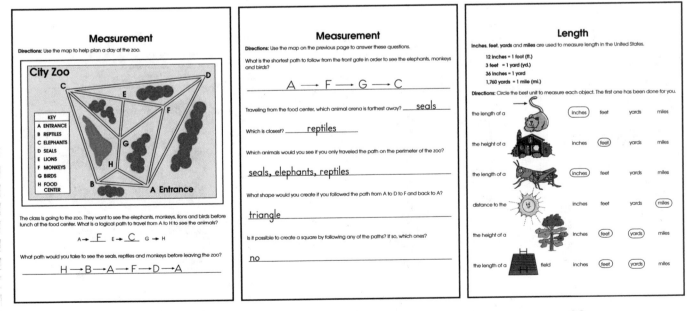

Length

Units of measure can be converted (changed) from one unit to another.

Example: The distance from the teacher's desk to the door is 24 feet.

24 ft. = __8__ yd.

Directions: Convert the units of measure using the previous page.

The distance from the plants to the computer is 5 yd.

5 yd. = __15__ ft.

The teacher's desk is 5 ft. long.

5 ft. = __60__ in.

The Reading Corner is 3 yd. wide.

3 yd. = __108__ in.

The distance from the computer to the door is 9 yd.

9 yd. = __27__ ft.

Classroom Map

Plants

Computer

Teacher's Desk

Door

Reading Corner

81

Length

Directions: Use a ruler to find the shortest paths. Round your measurement to the nearest quarter inch. Then convert to yards using the scale.

Scale: 1 inch = 100 yards

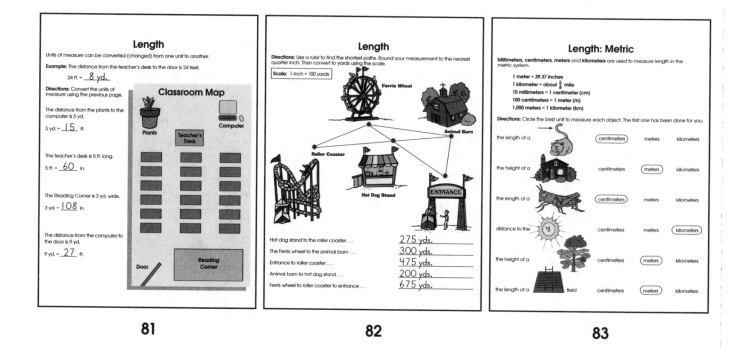

Ferris Wheel

Animal Barn

Roller Coaster

Hot Dog Stand

ENTRANCE

Hot dog stand to the roller coaster . . . __275 yds.__

The Ferris wheel to the animal barn . . . __300 yds.__

Entrance to roller coaster . . . __475 yds.__

Animal barn to hot dog stand . . . __200 yds.__

Ferris wheel to roller coaster to entrance . . . __675 yds.__

82

Length: Metric

Millimeters, centimeters, meters and kilometers are used to measure length in the metric system.

1 meter = 39.37 inches
1 kilometer = about $\frac{5}{8}$ mile
10 millimeters = 1 centimeter (cm)
100 centimeters = 1 meter (m)
1,000 meters = 1 kilometer (km)

Directions: Circle the best unit to measure each object. The first one has been done for you.

the length of a	(centimeters)	meters	kilometers
the height of a	centimeters	(meters)	kilometers
the length of a	(centimeters)	meters	kilometers
distance to the	centimeters	meters	(kilometers)
the height of a	centimeters	(meters)	kilometers
the length of a field	centimeters	(meters)	kilometers

83

Length: Metric

2.54 centimeters = 1 inch
1 millimeter = $\frac{1}{10}$ centimeter

Directions: Use a metric ruler to measure the length of each object.

$2\frac{1}{4}$ cm.

3 cm.

$10\frac{3}{4}$ cm.

$12\frac{3}{4}$ cm.

$7\frac{1}{4}$ cm.

$5\frac{1}{2}$ cm.

84

Weight

Ounces, pounds and tons are used to measure weight in the United States.

16 ounces = 1 pound (lb.)
2,000 pounds = 1 ton (tn.)

Directions: Circle the most reasonable estimate for the weight of each object. The first one has been done for you.

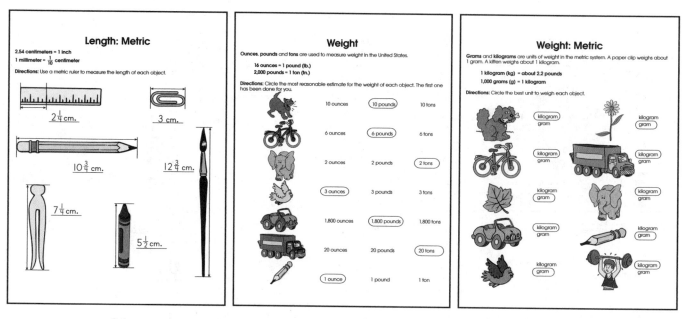

10 ounces	(10 pounds)	10 tons
6 ounces	(6 pounds)	6 tons
2 ounces	2 pounds	(2 tons)
(3 ounces)	3 pounds	3 tons
1,800 ounces	(1,800 pounds)	1,800 tons
20 ounces	20 pounds	(20 tons)
(1 ounce)	1 pound	1 ton

85

Weight: Metric

Grams and kilograms are units of weight in the metric system. A paper clip weighs about 1 gram. A kitten weighs about 1 kilogram.

1 kilogram (kg) = about 2.2 pounds
1,000 grams (g) = 1 kilogram

Directions: Circle the best unit to weigh each object.

(kilogram) / gram		kilogram / (gram)
(kilogram) / gram		(kilogram) / gram
kilogram / (gram)		(kilogram) / gram
(kilogram) / gram		(kilogram) / gram
kilogram / (gram)		(kilogram) / gram

86

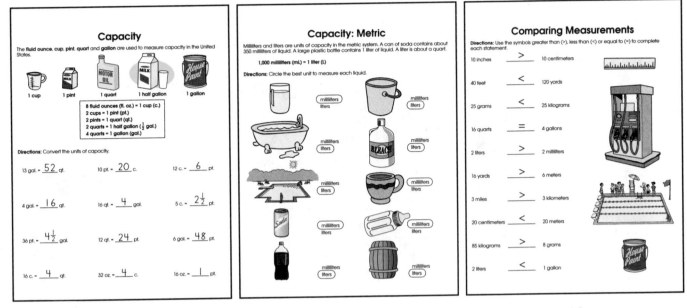

Capacity

The **fluid ounce**, **cup**, **pint**, **quart** and **gallon** are used to measure capacity in the United States.

1 cup   1 pint   1 quart   1 half gallon   1 gallon

8 fluid ounces (fl. oz.) = 1 cup (c.)
2 cups = 1 pint (pt.)
2 pints = 1 quart (qt.)
2 quarts = 1 half gallon ($\frac{1}{2}$ gal.)
4 quarts = 1 gallon (gal.)

Directions: Convert the units of capacity.

13 gal. = _52_ qt.   10 pt. = _20_ c.   12 c. = _6_ pt.

4 gal. = _16_ qt.   16 qt. = _4_ gal.   5 c. = _$2\frac{1}{2}$_ pt.

36 pt. = _$4\frac{1}{2}$_ gal.   12 qt. = _24_ pt.   6 gal. = _48_ pt.

16 c. = _4_ qt.   32 oz. = _4_ c.   16 oz. = _1_ pt.

87

Capacity: Metric

Milliliters and liters are units of capacity in the metric system. A can of soda contains about 350 milliliters of liquid. A large plastic bottle contains 1 liter of liquid. A liter is about a quart.

1,000 milliliters (mL) = 1 liter (L)

Directions: Circle the best unit to measure each liquid.

milliliters liters   milliliters liters

milliliters liters   milliliters liters

milliliters liters   milliliters liters

milliliters liters   milliliters liters

milliliters liters   milliliters liters

88

Comparing Measurements

Directions: Use the symbols greater than (>), less than (<) or equal to (=) to complete each statement.

10 inches __>__ 10 centimeters

40 feet __<__ 120 yards

25 grams __<__ 25 kilograms

16 quarts __=__ 4 gallons

2 liters __>__ 2 milliliters

16 yards __>__ 6 meters

3 miles __>__ 3 kilometers

20 centimeters __<__ 20 meters

85 kilograms __>__ 8 grams

2 liters __<__ 1 gallon

89

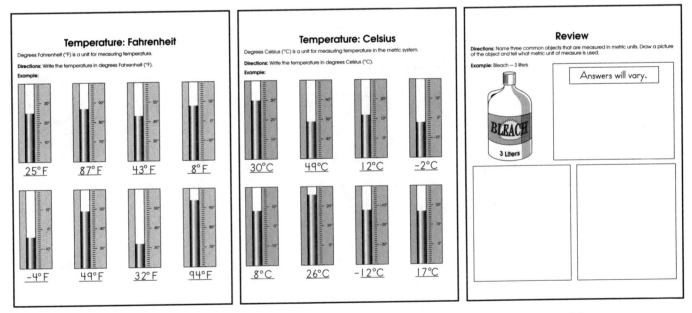

Temperature: Fahrenheit

Degrees Fahrenheit (°F) is a unit for measuring temperature.

Directions: Write the temperature in degrees Fahrenheit (°F).

Example:

_25°F_   _87°F_   _43°F_   _8°F_

_-4°F_   _49°F_   _32°F_   _94°F_

90

Temperature: Celsius

Degrees Celsius (°C) is a unit for measuring temperature in the metric system.

Directions: Write the temperature in degrees Celsius (°C).

Example:

_30°C_   _49°C_   _12°C_   _-2°C_

_8°C_   _26°C_   _-12°C_   _17°C_

91

Review

Directions: Name three common objects that are measured in metric units. Draw a picture of the object and tell what metric unit of measure is used.

Example: Bleach — 3 liters

Answers will vary.

BLEACH
3 Liters

92

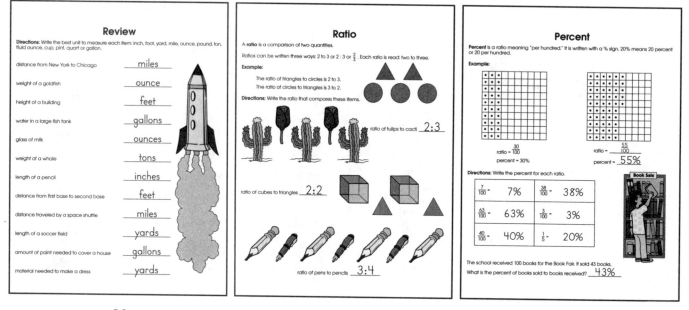

Review

Directions: Write the best unit to measure each item: inch, foot, yard, mile, ounce, pound, ton, fluid ounce, cup, pint, quart or gallon.

distance from New York to Chicago	miles
weight of a goldfish	ounce
height of a building	feet
water in a large fish tank	gallons
glass of milk	ounces
weight of a whale	tons
length of a pencil	inches
distance from first base to second base	feet
distance traveled by a space shuttle	miles
length of a soccer field	yards
amount of paint needed to cover a house	gallons
material needed to make a dress	yards

93

Ratio

A **ratio** is a comparison of two quantities.

Ratios can be written three ways: 2 to 3 or 2 : 3 or $\frac{2}{3}$. Each ratio is read: two to three.

Example:

The ratio of triangles to circles is 2 to 3.
The ratio of circles to triangles is 3 to 2.

Directions: Write the ratio that compares these items.

ratio of tulips to cacti   2:3

ratio of cubes to triangles   2:2

ratio of pens to pencils   3:4

94

Percent

Percent is a ratio meaning "per hundred." It is written with a % sign. 20% means 20 percent or 20 per hundred.

Example:

ratio = $\frac{30}{100}$
percent = 30%

ratio = $\frac{55}{100}$
percent = 55%

Directions: Write the percent for each ratio.

$\frac{7}{100}$ =	7%	$\frac{38}{100}$ =	38%
$\frac{63}{100}$ =	63%	$\frac{3}{100}$ =	3%
$\frac{40}{100}$ =	40%	$\frac{1}{5}$ =	20%

The school received 100 books for the Book Fair. It sold 43 books.
What is the percent of books sold to books received?   43%

95

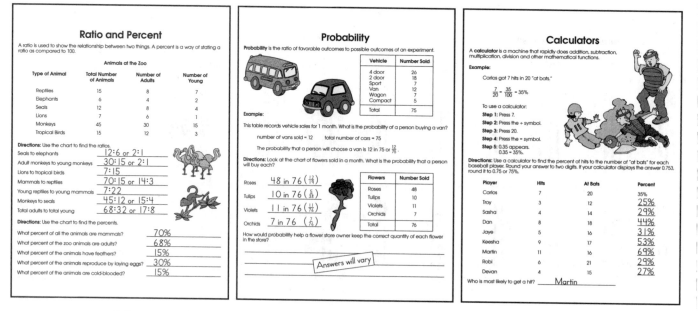

Ratio and Percent

A ratio is used to show the relationship between two things. A percent is a way of stating a ratio as compared to 100.

Animals at the Zoo

Type of Animal	Total Number of Animals	Number of Adults	Number of Young
Reptiles	15	8	7
Elephants	6	4	2
Seals	12	8	4
Lions	7	6	1
Monkeys	45	30	15
Tropical Birds	15	12	3

Directions: Use the chart to find the ratios.

Seals to elephants	12:6 or 2:1
Adult monkeys to young monkeys	30:15 or 2:1
Lions to tropical birds	7:15
Mammals to reptiles	70:15 or 14:3
Young reptiles to young mammals	7:22
Monkeys to seals	45:12 or 15:4
Total adults to total young	68:32 or 17:8

Directions: Use the chart to find the percents.

What percent of all the animals are mammals?	70%
What percent of the zoo animals are adults?	68%
What percent of the animals have feathers?	15%
What percent of the animals reproduce by laying eggs?	30%
What percent of the animals are cold-blooded?	15%

96

Probability

Probability is the ratio of favorable outcomes to possible outcomes of an experiment.

Vehicle	Number Sold
4 door	26
2 door	18
Sport	7
Van	12
Wagon	7
Compact	5
Total	75

Example:

This table records vehicle sales for 1 month. What is the probability of a person buying a van?

number of vans sold = 12   total number of cars = 75

The probability that a person will choose a van is 12 in 75 or $\frac{12}{75}$.

Directions: Look at the chart of flowers sold in a month. What is the probability that a person will buy each?

Roses	48 in 76 ($\frac{12}{19}$)
Tulips	10 in 76 ($\frac{5}{38}$)
Violets	11 in 76 ($\frac{11}{76}$)
Orchids	7 in 76 ($\frac{7}{76}$)

Flowers	Number Sold
Roses	48
Tulips	10
Violets	11
Orchids	7
Total	76

How would probability help a flower store owner keep the correct quantity of each flower in the store?

Answers will vary

97

Calculators

A **calculator** is a machine that rapidly does addition, subtraction, multiplication, division and other mathematical functions.

Example:

Carlos got 7 hits in 20 "at bats."

$\frac{7}{20} = \frac{35}{100} = 35\%$

To use a calculator:

Step 1: Press 7.
Step 2: Press the ÷ symbol.
Step 3: Press 20.
Step 4: Press the = symbol.
Step 5: 0.35 appears.
0.35 = 35%.

Directions: Use a calculator to find the percent of hits to the number of "at bats" for each baseball player. Round your answer to two digits. If your calculator displays the answer 0.753, round it to 0.75 or 75%.

Player	Hits	At Bats	Percent
Carlos	7	20	35%
Troy	3	12	25%
Sasha	4	14	29%
Dan	8	18	44%
Jaye	5	16	31%
Keesha	9	17	53%
Martin	11	16	69%
Robi	6	21	29%
Devan	4	15	27%

Who is most likely to get a hit?   Martin

98

Finding Percents

Find percent by dividing the number you have by the number possible.

Example:

15 out of 20 possible:
$$\begin{array}{r} 0.75 \\ 20\overline{)15.00} \\ \underline{140} \\ 100 \\ \underline{100} \end{array} = 75\%$$

Annie has been keeping track of the scores she earned on each spelling test during the grading period.

Directions: Find out each percentage grade she earned. The first one has been done for you.

Week	Number Correct		Total Number of Words	Score in Percent
1	14	(out of)	20	70%
2	16		20	80%
3	18		20	90%
4	12		15	80%
5	16		16	100%
6	17		18	94%
Review Test	51		60	85%

If Susan scored 5% higher than Annie on the review test, how many words did she get right?   54

Carrie scored 10% lower than Susan on the review test. How much did she spell correctly?   48

Of the 24 students in Annie's class, 25% had the same score as Annie. Only 10% had a higher score. What percent had a lower score?   65%

Is that answer possible?   no   65% of 24 is 15.6

Why?   cannot have a percent of a person

99

Locating Points on a Grid

Coordinates help locate places on maps at the point where their imaginary lines intersect.

Directions: Write the coordinates for the location of each object. The first one has been done for you.

Doll	3, T	Cat	15, N	Dog	13, B
Bike	15, V	Skateboard	7, L	Bird	4, C
Jump Rope	21, R	Baseball Glove	17, K	Rabbit	19, C

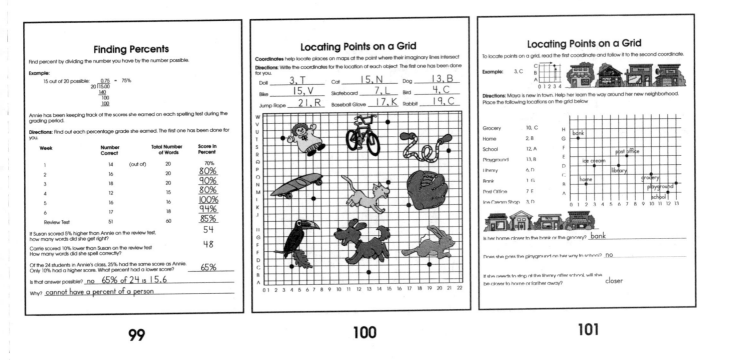

100

Locating Points on a Grid

To locate points on a grid, read the first coordinate and follow it to the second coordinate.

Example: 3, C

Directions: Maya is new in town. Help her learn the way around her new neighborhood. Place the following locations on the grid below.

Grocery	10, C
Home	2, B
School	12, A
Playground	13, B
Library	6, D
Bank	1, G
Post Office	7, E
Ice Cream Shop	3, D

Is her home closer to the bank or the grocery?   bank

Does she pass the playground on her way to school?   no

If she needs to stop at the library after school, will she be closer to home or farther away?   closer

101

Locating Points on a Grid

Directions: Draw the lines as directed from point to point for each graph.

Draw a line from:
- F,7 to D,1   • B,1 to A,8
- D,1 to L,6   • A,8 to D,11
- L,6 to N,8   • D,11 to F,9
- N,8 to M,3   • F,9 to F,7
- M,3 to F,1   • F,7 to L,9
- F,1 to G,4   • L,9 to L,6
- G,4 to E,4   • L,6 to F,7
- E,4 to B,1

Draw a line from:
- J, ■ to N, ◣
- N, ◣ to U, ◆
- U, ◣ to Z, ◆
- Z, ■ to X, ◆
- X, ◆ to U, ◣
- U, ◣ to S, ◉
- S, ◉ to N, ◣
- N, ◣ to N, ◉
- N, ◉ to J, ◉
- J, ■ to L, ▦
- L, ▦ to Y, ▦
- Y, ▦ to Z, ▦
- Z, ▦ to L, ▦
- L, ▦ to J, ■

102

Graphs

A **graph** is a drawing that shows information about changes in numbers.

Directions: Use the graph to answer the questions.

Line Graph   Temperatures for 1 Year

Which month was the coldest?   Dec.
Which month was the warmest?   July
Which three months were 40 degrees?   Jan., March, Nov.
How much warmer was it in May than October?   10°

Bar Graph   Home Runs

How many home runs did the Green team hit?   50
How many more home runs did the Green team hit than the Red team and Blue team combined?   20

103

Graphs

Directions: Read each graph and follow the directions.

Heights of Students

List the names of the students from the shortest to the tallest.
1. Tiffany   4. Louis
2. Michele   5. Jessie
3. Andy   6. Stephie

Lunches Bought

List how many lunches the students bought each day, from the day the most were bought to the least.
1. 92 (FRI)   4. 78 (THUR)
2. 84 (WED)   5. 72 (TUES)
3. 82 (MON)

Days of Outside Recess

List the months in the order of the most number of outside recesses to the least number.
1. June   6. March
2. May   7. November
3. April   8. February
4. September   9. January
5. October   10. December

104

Graphs

Directions: Complete the graph using the information in the table.

Student	Books read in February
Sue	20
Joe	8
Peter	12
Cindy	16
Dean	15
Carol	8

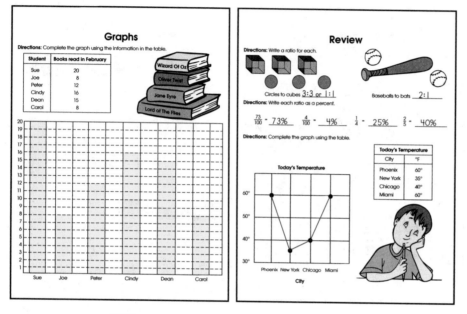

105

Review

Directions: Write a ratio for each.

Circles to cubes __3:3 or 1:1__

Baseballs to bats __2:1__

Directions: Write each ratio as a percent.

$\frac{73}{100}$ = __73%__ $\frac{4}{100}$ = __4%__ $\frac{1}{4}$ = __25%__ $\frac{2}{5}$ = __40%__

Directions: Complete the graph using the table.

Today's Temperature

Today's Temperature	
City	°F
Phoenix	60°
New York	35°
Chicago	40°
Miami	60°

106

Teaching Suggestions

Mathematics is a lifelong skill your child will never outgrow. Take advantage of opportunities to point out instances where math skills are applicable and necessary for daily tasks like balancing a checkbook, comparing costs or estimating the total at the grocery store.

The Four Basic Math Functions

Addition, subtraction, multiplication and division are the four basic math functions we use every day. Play oral counting games, counting by threes, fours, fives, sixes, sevens, etc. While tossing a ball back and forth, alternate turns counting by a given number. The person catching the ball says the next consecutive number in the sequence.

Count backwards by threes, fours, fives, etc., starting at different numbers each time.

Make up word problems with addition, subtraction, multiplication and division with your child while traveling in the car, waiting at the doctor's office or doing the dishes together. Use the situation to add relevance to the word problems. Include your child's name or friends' names in the problems.

Examples:

It is 375 miles to grandma's house. We have traveled 217 miles. How much farther do we need to drive?

It is 375 miles to grandma's house. We will take a break about half-way there. After how many miles will we take a break?

Family Math Challenge

Post a math question on the refrigerator. The first person to solve the question can select the next problem for the family. Plan a reward for the person who answers the most questions accurately during the week.

Math Maze

Plan a math maze by writing out math problems on large sheets of paper. On the back of each paper, write a clue telling where to find the next math page. Each math problem must be solved correctly before going on to the next one. Plan a small treat or reward at the end of the game.

Baking With Math

Baking and cooking are great opportunities for using math skills like measurement and fractions. Have your child help double or triple a recipe and calculate the ingredients needed.

Ask your child to create a chart showing grocery items labeled in metric and nonmetric units. Work together to change a recipe to metric measure.

Fractions

Let your child cut sandwiches into different fractions other than one-half or one-quarter.

Let your child cut a pizza into equal parts. Calculate the fraction of the pizza each member of the family can eat.

Percents

Help your child collect family data, like time spent sleeping, driving to work, etc. Ask him/her to create a graph showing time usage. Have him/her calculate the percent of a day or week spent doing various tasks.

Measurement

A tape measure is a great tool for measuring and a terrific learning tool. Let your child measure and compare the perimeter of various objects. Challenge him/her to find two unlike objects with exactly the same perimeter.

Money

Involve your child in opportunities dealing with money. Ask him/her to estimate prices on a shopping list, calculate change or double check a bill at a restaurant and calculate the tip.

Have your child determine how he/she spends his/her money. When he/she receives a money gift or allowance, ask him/her to figure the percent spent on savings, gifts and items purchased.

Help your child calculate the interest earned by putting aside a specific amount each week for a year. Help him/her work toward achieving a specific monetary goal.

When shopping, keep track of the number of items purchased and the total spent. Ask your child to determine the average cost.

Building

If you are planning to build a dog house, buy new carpeting or build a fence, involve your child in the planning by letting him/her help measure and calculate expenses. Create a supply list together. Use ads for prices to calculate the total cost. Explore alternate ways to complete the project at a lower cost. Many daily projects from planting a garden to reroofing the house involve mathematics. With all those opportunities available, you can keep your child involved in math every day.